Activate

Question · Progress · Succeed

2

Workbook: Higher

Including Diagnostic Pinchpoint activities

Jon Clarke
Philippa Gardom Hulme
Jo Locke

Assessment Editor
Dr Andrew Chandler-Grevatt

OXFORD
UNIVERSITY PRESS

Contents

Physics P2

Chapter 1 Electricity and magnetism

Chapter 2 Energy

Chapter 3 Motion and pressure

Introduction

Welcome to your *Activate* 2 Workbook. This Workbook contains lots of practice questions and activities to help you to progress through the course.

Each chapter from the *Activate* 2 Student Book is covered and includes a summary of all the content you need to know. Answers to all of the questions are in the back of the Workbook so you will be able to see how well you have answered them.

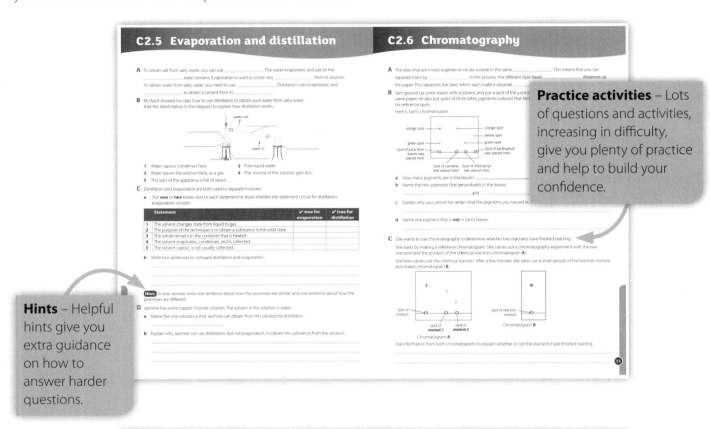

Practice activities – Lots of questions and activities, increasing in difficulty, give you plenty of practice and help to build your confidence.

Hints – Helpful hints give you extra guidance on how to answer harder questions.

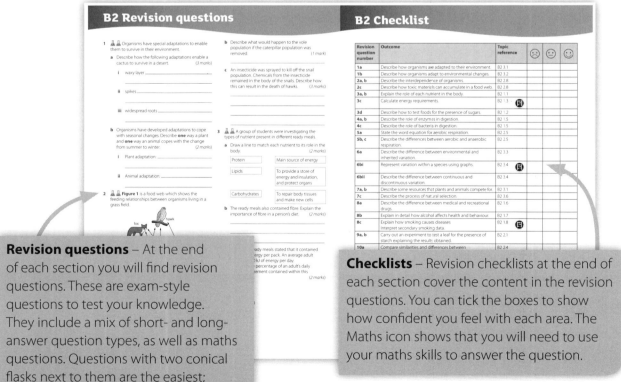

Revision questions – At the end of each section you will find revision questions. These are exam-style questions to test your knowledge. They include a mix of short- and long-answer question types, as well as maths questions. Questions with two conical flasks next to them are the easiest; questions with three flasks are harder.

Checklists – Revision checklists at the end of each section cover the content in the revision questions. You can tick the boxes to show how confident you feel with each area. The Maths icon shows that you will need to use your maths skills to answer the question.

Pinchpoints

A Pinchpoint is an idea or concept in science that can be challenging to learn. It is often difficult to say *why* these ideas are challenging to learn. The Pinchpoint intervention question at the end of each chapter focuses on a challenging idea from within the chapter. By answering the Pinchpoint question you will see whether you understand the concept or whether you have gone wrong. By doing the follow-up activity you will find out why you made the mistake and how to correct it.

Pinchpoint question – The Pinchpoint question is about a difficult concept from the chapter that students often get wrong. You should answer the Pinchpoint question and one follow-up activity. The Pinchpoint is multiple choice; answer the question by choosing a letter and then do the follow-up activity with the same letter.

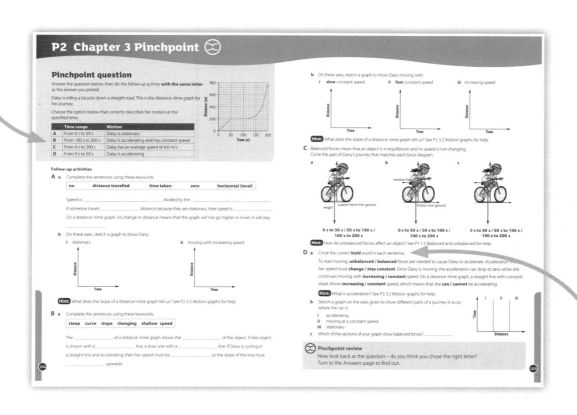

Pinchpoint follow-up – The follow-up activities will help you to better understand the difficult concept. If you got the Pinchpoint question right, the follow-up will develop your understanding further. If you got the Pinchpoint wrong, it will help you to see why you went wrong, and how to get it right next time.

B1.1 Nutrients

A Fill in the gaps to complete the sentences.

To remain healthy you must eat a _____ diet. This means eating food containing the right

_____ in the right amounts. These include _____ and _____ which

give you energy, _____ for growth and repair, _____ and _____ to

keep you healthy, and water and _____ to keep the food moving through your gut.

B Complete the table to explain the role of each nutrient in the body.

Nutrient	Role in the body
Carbohydrate	
Lipid	
Protein	
Vitamins and minerals	

C Fibre is not a nutrient. Explain why it is still an essential part of a healthy diet.

_____

_____

_____

D The food labels below are taken from a packet of baked beans and a pizza.

NUTRITION INFORMATION

Typical Composition	A 175g (6¼ oz) Serving Provides	100g (3½ oz) Provide
Energy	1567kJ/372kcal	893kJ/212kcal
Protein	20.2g	11.5g
Carbohydrate	47.6g	27.1g
of which sugars	7.7g	4.4g
Fat of which saturates	11.2g	6.4g
mono-unsaturates	6.3g	3.6g
polyunsaturates	3.7g	2.1g
	1.1g	0.6g
Fibre	3.3g	1.9g
Sodium	0.8g	0.5g

PIZZA

NUTRITION INFORMATION

Typical Values	Amount per 100g	Amount per Can
Energy	312kJ/75kcal	468kJ/113kcal
Protein	4.7g	7.1g
Carbohydrate (of which sugars)	13.6g (6.0g)	20.4g (9.0g)
Fat (of which saturates)	0.2g (Trace)	0.3g (Trace)
Fibre	3.7g	5.6g
Sodium	0.5g	0.7g

BAKED BEANS
in tomato sauce

For an average person, which would be the healthier choice? _____

Give 3 reasons for your answer.

1 _____

2 _____

3 _____

B1.2 Food tests

A Fill in the gaps to complete the sentences.

Scientists use _____ _____ to find out which nutrients are present in a food product.

_____ turns blue-black when _____ is present. Benedict's solution turns orange-

_____ if sugar is present. A solution of copper sulfate and sodium hydroxide solution will turn

_____ if _____ is present. Ethanol will turn _____ if lipids are present.

B Complete the table to show the chemical which should be used to test for the presence of each nutrient in a food solution.

Nutrient	Chemical
Starch	
	Ethanol
	Benedict's solution
Protein	

C You can also test a solid food sample for the presence of lipids. Describe this process.

_____

_____

_____

D A student tested three unknown food samples for the presence of different nutrients.

Sample	Colour of solution after adding...			
	Iodine	Benedict's solution	Ethanol	Copper sulfate and sodium hydroxide
X	Blue-black	Blue	Clear	Purple
Y	Orange-yellow	Red	Cloudy	Purple
Z	Orange-yellow	Red	Cloudy	Pale blue

Look at the results in the table and answer the following questions.

a Name which sample or samples contain protein. _____

b Name which sample or samples contain lipids. _____

c List the nutrients found in sample **Z**. _____

d Name which sample is most likely to be milk, and explain why. _____

Reasons: _____

e Give **one** reason why testing food for the presence of nutrients is important.

_____

B1.3 Unhealthy diet

A Fill in the gaps to complete the sentences.

Eating the wrong amount or wrong types of food is called _____. If the energy in the food you eat is

less than the energy you use, you will lose body mass and become _____. You are also likely to not

take in the correct amount of a vitamin or mineral. This is called a _____ and can make you ill. Not

eating enough food for prolonged periods is called _____. If you take in more energy than you use

by eating too much, you will gain body mass as _____, which is stored under the skin. Extremely

overweight people are said to be _____.

B Describe **two** conditions you are more likely to suffer from if you are underweight.

1 _____

2 _____

C Describe **two** conditions you are more likely to suffer from if you are overweight.

1 _____

2 _____

D The table below shows the energy requirements of some males and females.

Gender	Energy requirement per day (kJ)				
	Child	**Teenager**	**Office worker**	**Construction worker**	**Pregnant woman**
Male	8000	10 000	10 000	15 000	–
Female	8000	9000	9000	13 000	11 000

a i Calculate the difference in the amount of energy required by a male construction worker, and a male who works in an office job.

_____ kJ

ii Explain this difference.

_____

_____

b i Calculate the percentage increase in a female office worker's energy needs due to pregnancy.

_____ %

ii Explain this difference.

_____

_____

E Explain how an unhealthy diet can lead to obesity.

_____

_____

_____

B1.4 Digestive system

A Fill in the gaps to complete the sentences.

The group of organs that work together to break down food are called the _____

_____. Food enters the mouth and travels down your _____ into your

_____. Here it is mixed with _____ and digestive juices. As a result of

_____ small molecules of nutrients are produced which pass through the villi in the

_____ intestine into the blood. Water passes back into the body in the _____ intestine

leaving undigested food called faeces. This is stored in the _____ until it leaves the body through the

_____.

B Label the diagram of the digestive system.

mouth _____

_____

liver _____

pancreas

_____

_____

_____

anus

C Describe the function of the following organs in the digestive system.

Stomach _____

Large intestine _____

D Explain **two** ways the small intestine is adapted to its function.

1 _____

2 _____

E Explain why food needs to be digested.

_____

_____

_____

B1.5 Bacteria and enzymes in digestion

A Fill in the gaps to complete the sentences.

Some _____ living in your large intestine help you to remain healthy by making _____.

Special proteins called _____ help speed up digestion without being used up. They are a type

of _____. There are three main types – _____ which breaks down carbohydrate

molecules into _____ molecules, _____ which breaks down _____

into amino acids and _____ which breaks down lipid molecules into fatty acids and _____.

To help further with lipid digestion, _____ breaks the lipids into smaller droplets that are easier for

the enzymes to work on.

B a Identify the **two** correct statements about enzymes.

    W They are made of lipids

    X They speed up digestion

    Y They are known as biological catalysts

    Z They are used up during a reaction

  b Rewrite the two incorrect statements, so they read correctly:

_____

_____

C Each type of enzyme is involved in a different reaction. Complete the table to link the type of enzyme to the molecule it breaks down, and the molecules that are produced

Enzyme	Molecule it breaks down	Molecules produced
carbohydrase		
	lipid	
		amino acids

D There are some bacteria that live in your digestive system and improve your health.

  a Name where these bacteria are found.

_____

  b Name the food source for these bacteria.

_____

  c Explain how they improve your health.

_____

_____

B1.6 Drugs

A Fill in the gaps to complete the sentences.

Chemicals that affect the way your body works are called _____. _____ drugs are

taken for enjoyment whereas _____ drugs benefit your health. If you regularly take a drug, you

may develop an _____. If you then try to stop taking the drug, you may suffer from unpleasant

_____ _____, which make it harder to give up.

B Drugs can be divided into two main categories – medicinal and recreational drugs.
Describe what is meant by each type of drug and give a named example.

   a Medicinal drug _____

      Example _____

   b Recreational drug _____

      Example _____

C Complete the following sentences to describe how each of the following drugs affects your health.

   a Alcohol – damages _____

   b Tobacco – increases risk of _____ cancer

   c Caffeine – _____ the nervous system

D Explain why people take the following medicinal drugs.

   a Antibiotic _____

   b Paracetamol _____

E If your body gets used to the changes caused by a drug, you can become an addict.
Explain **two** problems associated with addiction to a recreational drug.

   1 _____

      _____

   2 _____

      _____

B1.7 Alcohol

A Fill in the gaps to complete the sentences.

Alcoholic drinks contain the drug _____. This acts on the _____ system and slows down body reactions; it is called a _____. Drinking too much alcohol can result in _____ and brain damage. Different alcoholic drinks contain different amounts of alcohol. 10 ml of alcohol is known as one _____ of alcohol. The government recommends that adults drink less than 2–3 units a day to remain healthy. People who are addicted to alcohol are known as _____.

B Long-term use of alcohol can lead to death.

    a Name the main two organs that are damaged by drinking alcohol.

        1 _____

        2 _____

    b The graph shows the number of alcohol-related deaths in UK males between 1991 and 2008.

    Using data from the graph, describe the trend shown.

    _____

    _____

C Alcohol has an effect on pregnancy and conception.

    a Explain why men should reduce their alcohol intake if they are planning to have a child.

    _____

    _____

    b Explain why a pregnant woman should avoid alcohol.

    _____

    _____

    _____

B1.8 Smoking

A Fill in the gaps to complete the sentences.

Smoking increases the risk of many conditions such as lung _____ and _____ attacks.

The risk of someone else developing one of these conditions also increases if they breathe in the smoke. This is

called _____ smoking. Tobacco smoke contains many harmful chemicals such as tar which narrows

the _____, carbon _____ which reduces the amount of _____ the

blood can carry, and nicotine. As well as being addictive nicotine is a _____ which makes the heart

beat faster. Smoking in pregnancy affects fetal development and can cause _____.

B Tobacco smoke contains over 4000 chemicals, many of which are harmful.
Describe the effects of the following components of tobacco smoke on the body.

a Tar _____

b Carbon monoxide _____

c Nicotine _____

C Carlos studies the graph opposite.

He draws a conclusion based on the data: If you smoke then you will get lung cancer.

Correct his conclusion.

_____

_____

_____

_____

_____

_____

D Explain how smoking increases your risk of suffering from a respiratory infection.

Hint: think about the ciliated cells in your airways.

_____

_____

_____

E Explain why a pregnant woman should avoid smoking.

_____

Pinchpoint question

Answer the question below, then do the follow-up activity **with the same letter** as the answer you picked.

Which of the following statements best describes the structure and function of the small intestine?

A Villi present in the small intestine move food particles along the intestine, speeding up absorption.

B The small intestine is specially adapted for its sole function of absorption, so enzymes are not present.

C The small intestine has a large surface area to maximise the rate of absorption.

D The wall of the small intestine is smooth to maximise the rate of absorption.

Follow-up activities

A Circle the correct bold terms in the sentences below to describe how food is moved along the intestine.

Fat / fibre in your food is not digested. This adds **liquid / bulk** to the food.

Muscles / ligaments in the **wall / centre** of the intestine **push against / pull** this mass, forcing the food along the intestine.

This process can be modelled by **sucking on a straw / squeezing a tube of toothpaste**.

Small **soluble / insoluble** molecules produced as a result of digestion are absorbed through the **small / large** intestine wall into the blood stream. The villi present increase the surface area of the small intestine. This **prevents / speeds up** absorption.

Eventually only a solid waste of undigested food is left. This is called **urine / feces** which is stored in the **rectum / bladder** until it can be removed from the body.

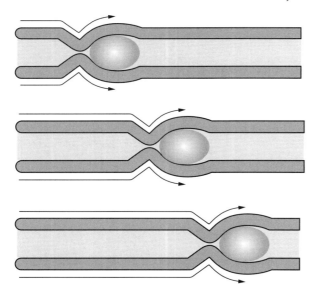

Hint: Look at the diagram to help you complete the sentences. See B2 1.4 Digestive system for help.

B Enzymes in the body help to digest large food molecules. There are three main groups of enzymes.

a Complete the following sentences to describe the role of each enzyme.

Carbohydrase enzymes break down _____ into _____

Protease enzymes break down _____ into _____

Lipase enzymes break down _____ into _____

b Complete the following table to show where enzymes are found in the body. Add a tick for each place the enzyme is found.

Enzyme	Mouth	Stomach	Small intestine
Carbohydrase			
Protease			
Lipase			

Hint: There is only one type of enzyme found in the mouth. It breaks down large carbohydrate molecules into sugars. See B2 1.5 Bacteria and enzymes in digestion for help.

C Coeliac disease is caused by an abnormal immune system reaction to the protein gluten, which is found in foods such as bread, pasta, cereals and biscuits. It causes the immune system to mistake healthy cells and substances for harmful ones and produces antibodies against them (antibodies usually fight off bacteria and viruses). The antibodies produced for people with coeliac disease cause the surface of their intestine to become inflamed. This inflammation flattens villi, reducing their ability to help with digestion.

a Name the main food group that contains foods containing gluten.

_____

b Suggest and explain the symptoms of coeliac disease.

_____

_____

_____

_____

Hint: Think about the function of villi. What would happen if the villi were removed? See B2 1.4 Digestive system for help.

D The wall of the small intestine is covered in tiny projections called villi.

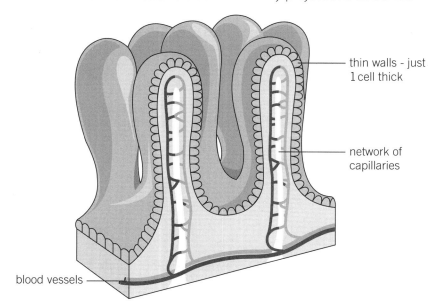

thin walls - just
1 cell thick

network of
capillaries

blood vessels

a Draw a line to match each sentence starter to its correct ending.

i Walls of intestine are thin

1 to create a large surface area.

ii Walls of intestine are covered in lots of villi

2 to transport absorbed food molecules to where they are needed.

iii Villi have a rich blood supply

3 to minimise the diffusion distance.

b Explain how a constant flow of blood through the villi maximises diffusion.

_____

_____

_____

Hint: The rate of diffusion is affected by distance, the difference in concentration and the surface area in contact. See B2 1.4 Digestive system for help.

Pinchpoint review

Now look back at the question – do you think you chose the right letter?
Turn to the Answers page to find out.

B2.1 Photosynthesis

A Fill in the gaps to complete the sentences.

Plants and _____ are called _____ because they make their own food by the process

of _____. Animals are called _____ as they have to eat other organisms to survive.

During photosynthesis, carbon dioxide and _____ are converted into oxygen and _____

using energy from the Sun. This light energy is absorbed by _____ in chloroplasts.

B Plants and algae both produce their own food by the process of photosynthesis.

   a Complete the word equation for photosynthesis.

                                                 _____

     carbon dioxide + _____ $\longrightarrow$ glucose + _____

   b Circle the products of photosynthesis.

   c Underline the reactants of photosynthesis.

C Some of the sugar made during photosynthesis is stored as starch in leaves. Leaves can be tested for the presence of starch.

   a The statements below can be reordered to describe how to test a leaf for the presence of starch. Read the statements and write down the order of statements you think will give the best description.

     Correct order: ☐ ☐ ☐ ☐ ☐ ☐ ☐

     1 Put the boiling tube into the beaker of hot water and leave until most of the chlorophyll has been removed.

     2 Turn off the Bunsen burner.

     3 Spread the leaf on a white tile and add a few drops of iodine.

     4 Place a leaf in the beaker of boiling water and leave for two minutes.

     5 Boil a beaker of water using a Bunsen burner.

     6 Remove the leaf from the ethanol and swill in water.

     7 Remove the leaf and place into a boiling tube containing ethanol.

   b Describe a positive result for the presence of starch.

   _____

D Explain how the following enter a plant to be used in photosynthesis.

   a Carbon dioxide _____

   b Water _____

   c Light _____

E Explain why photosynthesis is important for all organisms in a food chain.

_____

_____

_____

Hint: For help with this question, look at B2 2.7 Food chains and webs.

B2.2 Leaves

A Fill in the gaps to complete the sentences.

Photosynthesis in a plant mainly takes place in the _____, though a small amount occurs in the stems.

The underneath of a leaf contains tiny holes called _____ which allow _____ _____ to

diffuse into the leaf and _____ to diffuse out. Water is carried to the leaf in the _____. Most

photosynthesis occurs in the cells of the _____ layer as most light reaches this layer. Therefore, these

cells are full of _____.

B Label the diagram of the cross-section through a leaf.

C Describe the function of the following parts of a leaf.

   a Veins _____

   b Waxy layer _____

   c Guard cells _____

   d Stomata _____

D Explain the distribution of chloroplasts in a leaf and their role in photosynthesis.

_____

_____

_____

E Explain why most leaves are thin and have a large surface area.

_____

_____

_____

B2.3 Plant minerals

A Fill in the gaps to complete the sentences.

To stay healthy, plants need to absorb _____ from the soil. For healthy growth, plants need

four minerals – _____ to make chlorophyll, _____ for healthy leaves and flowers,

_____ for healthy growth and _____ for healthy roots. If a plant does not get enough

of a mineral it is said to have a _____ and will not grow properly. To prevent this occurring, farmers

add chemicals called _____ to the soil.

B Draw a line to match each mineral to its use in the plant, and describe the plant's appearance if this mineral
is deficient.

Mineral	Function	Deficiency symptoms
Nitrate	Making chlorophyll	
Phosphate	Healthy growth	
Potassium	Healthy roots	
Magnesium	Healthy leaves and flowers	

C Deficiency in the mineral potassium can result in yellow leaves.

a Name one other mineral deficiency that results in yellow leaves.

_____

b Explain how the deficiency results in yellow leaves.

_____

_____

D A scientist measured the height of a number of tomato plant seedlings after a month of growth. Each received the
same amount of water and light but received different types of mineral supplement.

Three mineral supplements were tested, labelled A, B, and C. One sample contained nitrogen, phosphorus, and
magnesium; one sample contained nitrogen and magnesium; and one sample contained no useful minerals. Five
seedlings were placed in each supplement.

a The height of seedlings grown using supplement A was measured. The results are shown below.

24.6 cm   32 cm   31.5 cm   34 cm   32.4 cm

Calculate the mean height of these seedlings.

_____

b The mean height of seedlings grown in supplement B was 20.4 cm, and in supplement C was 21.2 cm.

Is there enough evidence to work out which plant received a 'dummy' supplement, containing no useful
minerals? Explain your answer.

_____

_____

B2.4 Chemosynthesis

A Fill in the gaps to complete the sentences.

Some species of _____ make their own food by the process of _____. They use the

energy released by _____ reactions to make _____. One example of chemosynthetic

bacteria is _____ bacteria living at the bottom of the _____ near volcanic vents.

B Complete the following sentences about the process of chemosynthesis.

The source of energy for chemosynthesis is _____

The product of chemosynthesis is _____

A reactant often used in chemosynthesis is _____

Hint: The reactant often used in chemosynthesis is a **gas**.

C Bacteria that perform chemosynthesis are called chemosynthetic bacteria.

Name **two** examples of where chemosynthetic bacteria are found and the chemical source they use for chemosynthesis.

1 _____

_____

2 _____

_____

D Complete the following table to compare the processes of photosynthesis and chemosynthesis.

In the first row, name the energy source. For the remaining rows, use the terms **yes**, **no**, or **sometimes**.

Process	Chemosynthesis	Photosynthesis
Energy source		
Water required?		
Carbon dioxide required?		
Glucose produced?		

E Tubeworms and sulfur bacteria can both be found near deep sea vents.

Explain why they form a mutualistic relationship.

_____

_____

_____

_____

B2.5 Aerobic respiration

A Fill in the gaps to complete the sentences.

Energy is released in your cells by _____ _____. During this process, _____

and oxygen react inside your _____ to release energy. The waste products carbon dioxide and

_____ are also produced.

Glucose is produced when _____ are broken down during digestion. Glucose is transported around

your body in the _____ in the blood. It then _____ into cells.

Oxygen is also transported by the blood. It binds to the _____ in red blood cells.

B Complete the word equation for aerobic respiration.

glucose + _____ ⟶ water + _____ _____ (+ energy)

C Respiration takes place inside your cells.

a Name the component of the cell in which respiration occurs. _____

b Explain why muscle cells contain large numbers of this component.

_____

_____

D Imagine you have been asked to plan an investigation to measure the effect of exercise on breathing rates.

a List the following variables in your investigation:

i independent variable _____

ii dependent variable _____

iii control variable _____

b Explain what you think will happen.

_____

_____

_____

E Explain how the following reactants of aerobic respiration get into your cells.

Include the key words below in your answer.

diffuse	alveoli	plasma	haemoglobin

a glucose

_____

_____

_____

b oxygen

_____

_____

_____

B2.6 Anaerobic respiration

A Fill in the gaps to complete the sentences.

When your body respires without oxygen it is called _____ _____. This produces

_____ _____ which can build up in your muscles and cause cramp. To break

down the acid, you have to breathe in extra oxygen. This is called an _____ _____.

Microorganisms such as yeast carry out a type of anaerobic respiration called _____. In this reaction,

carbon dioxide and _____ are produced.

B Write down the word equation for anaerobic respiration in animal cells.

_____ ⟶ _____

C The table shows some statements about respiration.
Tick **one** column in each row to show which statements are true for each type of respiration.

	✓ if true for aerobic respiration	✓ if true for anaerobic respiration
Glucose is a reactant		
Oxygen is a reactant		
Carbon dioxide is produced		
Lactic acid is produced		
Water is produced		

D **a** Give **two** reasons why animals normally carry out aerobic respiration.

   1 _____

   2 _____

   b Give **one** reason why animals respire anaerobically.

   _____

E Yeast is an important microorganism in the food and drink industry.

   a Write down the name of the type of anaerobic respiration it performs.

   _____

   b Explain how yeast is used to make beer.

   _____

   _____

   c Explain how yeast is used to make bread.

   _____

   _____

   _____

B2.7 Food chains and webs

A Fill in the gaps to complete the sentences.

A _____ _____ is a diagram that shows the transfer of _____ between organisms.

The first organism is always a _____. It transfers energy from the Sun into glucose by _____.

The other organisms in the chain are _____. They eat other organisms to gain energy. An animal that is

eaten by another organism is called a _____ organism. The animal that eats it is called a _____.

Most animals have more than one food source. This can be shown on a _____ _____. These

diagrams show a set of _____ food chains.

B Describe the difference between a food chain and a food web.

_____

_____

_____

C This food web shows the relationships between organisms in a garden.

a Using information from the food web, draw a food chain with four links.

_____ → _____ → _____ → _____

b On your food chain, label which organism is each of the following:

| producer | carnivore | herbivore | predator | prey |

D Explain why many food chains have no more than four links.

_____

_____

_____

B2.8 Disruption to food chains and webs

A Fill in the gaps to complete the sentences.

Living organisms depend on other organisms to survive. This is called _____. The number of organisms of a particular species in an area is called a _____. If the size of one population increases, it can change the size of another population. For example, if a producer population increases, the consumer population may

_____.

Toxic chemicals can build up in the organisms in a food chain. This is called _____.

B Look at this food chain found in the sea: plankton ⟶ small fish ⟶ shark

Mercury is found in low levels in the sea, which is taken in by plankton. Mercury is toxic to humans.

Pregnant women are advised not to eat shark meat due to the high levels of mercury sometimes found in sharks; however, this advice does not apply to eating smaller fish that live in the same area. Explain why.

_____

_____

_____

_____

C This graph shows what happened to the population of native ocean fish when lionfish (a new predator) was introduced to an area.

Explain the trends shown in the population sizes in the graph.

_____

_____

_____

_____

_____

_____

Key
— Prey
···· Predator

Population density

Lionfish introduction

Time

D Wolves have recently been reintroduced into Yellowstone National Park in the USA. Use the information below to explain how the interdependence of organisms has caused changes to rivers within the national park.

- Elks feed on willow trees.
- Elks are eaten by wolves.
- Beavers eat willow and use the branches to make dams.

_____

_____

_____

B2.9 Ecosystems

A Fill in the gaps to complete the sentences.

The place where an organism lives is called a _____. The organisms living in a particular area are called a

_____. The organisms and the area where they live is known as an _____. Different organisms

living together in the same place at the same time are said to _____. This is possible because they have

their own _____ – a particular place or role within the ecosystem.

B A group of students looked at the organisms present in an oak tree ecosystem. They found birds, ants, squirrels, woodlice, and slugs living on the oak trees.

a Complete the sentences below to describe differences in the organisms' niches.

Birds and squirrels both live in the tree canopy. They can co-exist as they have different _____

_____ .

Squirrels and woodlice can co-exist as they are found in different _____.

b In the sentences above, circle the habitat and underline the community.

C A scientist investigated the distribution of plants at different distances from a hedgerow. Using the equipment below, they took measurements every 5 metres from the hedgerow.

wire or string   metal or wooden frame

a i Name the piece of equipment the scientist used. _____

ii Name the type of habitat the scientist is investigating. _____

b Suggest one reason for the change in distribution that the scientist observes.

_____

c Explain why the measurements are unbiased.

_____

_____

Pinchpoint question

Answer the question below, then do the follow-up activity **with the same letter** as the answer you picked.

Which of the following statements best describes the process of photosynthesis?

A   Can be represented by the word equation glucose + oxygen → carbon dioxide + water.

B   The method by which plants inhale carbon dioxide and exhale oxygen.

C   The process by which plants use water and minerals from the soil to make glucose.

D   The production of glucose and oxygen from carbon dioxide and water.

Follow-up activities

A   The following paragraph describes what happens in photosynthesis. Read the paragraph then complete the activities listed below.

Plants make food by the process of photosynthesis. Photosynthesis is a chemical reaction in which plants take in carbon dioxide and water and convert them into glucose. This provides the plant with food. Oxygen is also produced, which is released back into the atmosphere. This is used by plants and animals in respiration.

a   Underline the **two** reactants of photosynthesis.

b   Circle the **two** products of photosynthesis.

c   Complete the word equation for photosynthesis.

_____ + _____ $\xrightarrow{\hspace{2cm}}$ _____ + _____

(**Hint:**) Reactants are the starting substances in a chemical reaction. See C1 3.2 Word equations and B2 2.1 Photosynthesis for help.

B   Circle the correct bold terms in the sentences below to describe how plants exchange gases, and their uses in the plant.

Plants take in air containing oxygen and carbon dioxide through their **lungs / leaves**. The gases diffuse into the

plant through tiny pores called **stomata / alveoli**.

Both carbon dioxide and oxygen are used for different processes inside the plant. Photosynthesis requires

carbon dioxide / oxygen, while **carbon dioxide / oxygen** is needed for respiration.

Plants do release some oxygen from their leaves as it is produced as a result of **respiration / photosynthesis**.

However, it is not released through breathing. It passes out of the leaf through the **stomata / alveoli**, again

through the process of diffusion. Some of the oxygen remains in the plant and is used in respiration to produce

glucose / energy.

(**Hint:**) Think about the structure of a leaf. How is it adapted for gas exchange? See B2 2.1 Photosynthesis and B2 2.2 Leaves for help.

C A group of students grew some seedlings in petri dishes on a warm window sill. The table below shows their observations after four weeks.

Dish	Conditions	Observations
1	Seedling roots placed into cotton wool ball	Shrivelled appearance, dead
2	Seedling roots placed into cotton wool ball soaked in distilled (pure) water. Water replaced every two days.	Shoots with leaves, some spindly and some yellow, plant alive and growing
3	Seedling roots placed into dry, mineral rich soil	Shrivelled appearance, dead
4	Seedling roots placed into mineral rich soil and distilled water. Water replaced every two days.	Green shoots and leaves, plant alive and growing

a Name the dish where the plants grew best. _____

b Explain the observations gained by the group of students.

_____

_____

_____

_____

Hint: Think about the word equation for photosynthesis. What reactants are needed? See B2 2.1 Photosynthesis and B2 2.3 Plant minerals for help.

D Plants photosynthesise to make glucose. This is used for energy, to enable the plant to grow. To maximise growth farmers often grow plants in a greenhouse. This allows them to control the environment that the plant is growing in.

a List **three** factors which could affect the rate at which photosynthesis occurs.

1 _____

2 _____

3 _____

b A group of students investigated how light intensity affected the rate of photosynthesis. These are their results.

Relative light intensity	1	2	3	4	5	6	7	8
Relative rate of photosynthesis	3.0	6.0	7.5	8.0	8.5	9.0	9.0	9.0

Plot the students' data on the graph paper below.

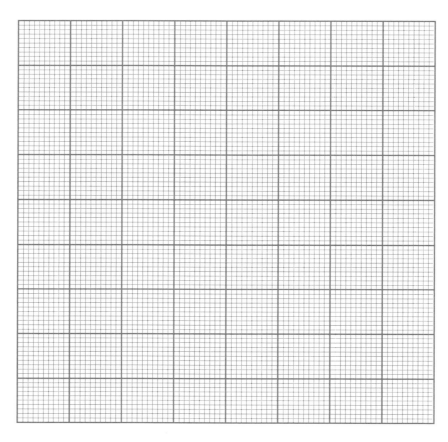

c Describe the trend shown by the graph.

_____

_____

d At a relative light intensity of 0, the relative rate of photosynthesis was also 0. Explain why.

_____

_____

e Suggest and explain the relative rate of photosynthesis at a relative light intensity of 10.

_____

_____

Hint: Think about the word equation for photosynthesis. To maximise the rate of photosynthesis you need to maximise the availability of the reactants. See B2 2.1 Photosynthesis for help.

⊗ **Pinchpoint review**
Now look back at the question – do you think you chose the right letter?
Turn to the Answers page to find out.

B3.1 Competition and adaptation

A Fill in the gaps to complete the sentences.

In order to survive, plants and animals compete for _____ such as water and space. Animals also

compete for _____ to reproduce, and for _____. Plants compete for water and for

_____ for photosynthesis and _____ for healthy growth. To help them survive, plants

and animals have special characteristics called _____.

B Give **three** resources that plants compete for and what the plants need these for.

1 _____

2 _____

3 _____

C Animals also compete for resources.

a Name **one** resource other than food and water that an animal species competes for.

_____

b Describe why it needs this resource.

_____

c A new species of animal is introduced to the area, which competes for food.

Suggest and explain what could happen to the original animal population.

_____

_____

D Look at the diagram of a cactus.

Label **three** adaptations on the cactus and explain how each adaptation helps the cactus to survive in a desert.

B3.2 Adapting to change

A Fill in the gaps to complete the sentences.

Plants and animals have to cope with changes in their _____. For example, in winter, trees lose their

_____ and sheep grow thicker _____. Sudden changes such as fire or disease mean that only the

best _____ organisms survive and reproduce.

When a predator has only one main food source, there is an _____ between the predator and prey

populations. A change in the population of one directly causes a change in the other. For example, if the prey

population increases, the predator population _____ as they have more _____, meaning more

stay alive to reproduce.

B A population of rabbits lives in a field. Foxes are predators of rabbits.

Study the graph opposite.

a Label the lines to show which represents the population of foxes and which represents the population of rabbits.

b Tick the boxes next to all the correct statements.

W As the number of rabbits goes up, the number of foxes goes down. ☐

X When the number of rabbits goes down, the amount of grass in the field decreases. ☐

Y As fox numbers increase, the population of rabbits decreases. ☐

Z As the number of rabbits increases, so does the number of foxes. ☐

c Explain the trends you have identified.

_____

_____

C Explain **one** way a plant and **one** way an animal copes with the seasons changing from summer to winter.

Plant _____

_____

Animal _____

_____

D Explain how competition for a food source can lead to changes in the population of that species.

_____

_____

_____

B3.3 Variation

A Fill in the gaps to complete the sentences.

Organisms from the same _____ can reproduce to produce fertile offspring. Differences in their

characteristics are known as _____. This can be caused by _____ variation –

characteristics that have been passed on from their parents such as eye colour. It can also be caused by an

organism's surroundings – _____ variation; for example, the amount of light a plant receives.

However, many characteristics are affected by both causes.

B Variation between individuals may be due to inherited variation, environmental variation, or both.

Draw a line to match each human variation to its cause.

Variation   **Cause**

| eye colour |

| height | | inherited |

| accent |
                                                              | environment |
| pierced ears |

| blood group | | a combination of both |

| skin colour |

C Describe the difference between environmental and inherited variation.

_____

_____

_____

D A cat had eight kittens.

  a Explain why the kittens did not all look identical.

_____

_____

_____

  b Explain why the differences in the kittens' appearance became greater as they got older.

_____

_____

_____

A Fill in the gaps to complete the sentences.

Characteristics that can only result in certain values show _____ variation; for example, gender. This

type of variation should be plotted on a _____ _____ . Characteristics that can result

in any value within a range show _____ variation; for example, height. This type of variation should

be plotted on a _____ .

B Sort the following characteristics into those which show continuous variation and those which show discontinuous variation.

leg length	blood group	leaf surface area	flower colour	fish mass	number of spots

Continuous variation	Discontinuous variation

C Describe what is meant by a characteristic that shows:

a Continuous variation

_____

b Discontinuous variation

_____

D A group of students investigated the height tomato plants grow to over a six-week period.

a **i** What type of variation is plant height? _____

ii What is the cause of the variation in plant height?

_____

_____

_____

b Name the type of graph they should use to display their measurements.

_____

B3.5 Inheritance

A Fill in the gaps to complete the sentences.

You inherit characteristics from your parents through genetic material found in the _____ of your

cells. Genetic material is made up of the chemical _____ – this contains all the information needed

to make an organism. In the nucleus, this chemical is organised into long strands called _____.

Each strand is divided into sections called _____. Each section contains the information needed to

produce a characteristic.

B Annotate the diagram to explain how characteristics are passed on from parents to their offspring.
Use the following terms:

sperm	egg	nucleus	chromosome	23	46

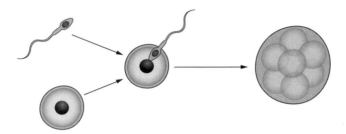

C Explain the function of a gene.

_____

_____

D Explain how the work of different teams of scientists led to the discovery of the structure of DNA.

_____

_____

_____

_____

B3.6 Natural selection

A Fill in the gaps to complete the sentences.

All organisms living today have _____ from a common ancestor. This process has taken

_____ of years and has occurred as a result of _____ _____.

The organisms most adapted to their environment _____ and reproduce, passing on the

_____ which code for these characteristics to their offspring. The remains of organisms that lived

millions of years ago, called _____, provide evidence for evolution.

B The statements below can be reordered to describe how a species evolves through the process of natural selection. Read the statements and write down the order of statements you think will give the best description.

Correct order ☐ ☐ ☐ ☐ ☐ ☐

1 Process is repeated over many generations.
2 Genes which code for advantageous characteristics are passed on to offspring.
3 New species can evolve where all organisms have the adaptations.
4 Organisms in a species show variation.
5 More organisms within the species have the advantageous characteristic.
6 The organisms with the characteristics that are best suited to the environment survive and reproduce. Less well-adapted organisms die.

C Fossils provide important evidence for evolution.

a Describe what a fossil is.

_____

b Explain how fossils provide evidence for evolution.

_____

D Using a named example, explain how natural selection leads to evolution.

_____

_____

_____

_____

B3.7 Extinction

A Fill in the gaps to complete the sentences.

The range of organisms living in an area is called _____. Destruction of _____ and

outbreaks of _____ can cause a reduction in biodiversity and can lead to a species becoming

_____. This is where there are no individuals of a species living anywhere in the world. When only a

small number of a species exist, the species is said to be _____. One way scientists try to ensure plant

species survive is through storing genetic material in a _____ _____.

B There are many species of plants and animals in the world that are endangered. One way that scientists are trying
to prevent them becoming extinct is by using gene banks.

   a Describe how gene banks are used to try to prevent extinction.

     _____

     _____

   b There are many different types of gene bank. Describe **two** different gene banks.

     1 _____

        _____

        _____

     2 _____

        _____

        _____

C Explain **three** factors that could lead to a species becoming extinct.

   1 _____

      _____

   2 _____

      _____

   3 _____

      _____

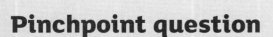

Pinchpoint question

Answer the question below, then do the follow-up activity **with the same letter** as the answer you picked.

Which of the following statements best describes the process of evolution by natural selection?

A Process by which an organism with an advantageous adaptation survives and passes on the characteristic. The entire next generation are adapted and have the beneficial characteristic.

B Process by which a species changes over many generations to become better adapted to its environment.

C Evolution involves changes to a species. This process always takes millions of years.

D Process by which an organism changes to become better suited to its environment.

Follow-up activities

A In an area of land, there are 15 000 organisms of species X, a predator. For species X, the faster the organism the more chance it has of survival, as it is more able to catch its prey.

The table below shows how the species evolves over time to become faster. The overall population of species X remains constant.

Generation	1	2	5	10	100
Number of individuals who can run at over 40 km/h	75	150	500	1000	5000

   a Calculate the proportion of offspring in the original generation that can run faster than 40 km/h. _____

   b Calculate the proportion of offspring in generation 100 that can run faster than 40 km/h. _____

   c Explain the difference in your answers to parts **a** and **b**.

_____

_____

_____

Hint: To calculate a percentage, divide the number in the generation by the total population. To help you explain in part **c**, see B2 3.6 Natural selection.

B Pathogens such as bacteria and viruses reproduce very rapidly and can evolve in a relatively short time. Explain how the evolution of bacteria can lead to antibiotic resistance.

_____

_____

_____

_____

_____

_____

Hint: Due to variation, some bacteria in a species may be naturally resistant to an antibiotic. See B2 3.6 Natural Selection for help.

C **a** Choose the appropriate words from the box below to complete the following sentences which describe how peppered moths evolved. You will need to use some words more than once.

camouflaged	pale	increasing	eaten	dark	reproduced	soot	decreasing

There are two types of peppered moth: pale moths and dark moths. Before the industrial revolution there

were more _____ moths as these were _____ against the pale tree bark;

_____ moths were seen and _____. More _____ moths survived

and _____ increasing the number of these moths in the population.

After the industrial revolution, many trees in urban areas were covered in _____. The

_____ moths were now more _____ so survived and reproduced. This resulted

in the number of pale moths _____, and the number of dark moths _____. Most

moths in the population were now _____.

b The first dark peppered moth was recorded in Manchester in 1848. By 1895, 98% of peppered moths in the city were black. Calculate the number of years over which this example of evolution took place.

_____.

Hint: In order to pass on a characteristic an organism needs to survive and reproduce. See B2 3.6 Natural selection for help.

D The statements below describe how the giraffe species has evolved over time to have longer necks. Add a picture in the box next to each statement to show what is occurring.

1	2	3

Originally there were short- and long-necked giraffes within the population

Long-necked giraffes had an advantage as they could reach the taller trees

More long-necked giraffes survived. Short-necked giraffes died due to a lack of food

4	5

Long-necked giraffes reproduced, passing on genes for long necks

After many generations, all giraffes have long necks

Hint: Include images of several giraffes in your pictures, as evolution applies to a species, not an individual organism. See B2 3.6 Natural selection for help.

Pinchpoint review

Now look back at the question – do you think you chose the right letter?
Turn to the Answers page to find out.

B2 Revision questions

1 ⚗️⚗️ Organisms have special adaptations to enable them to survive in their environment.

  a Describe how the following adaptations enable a cactus to survive in a desert. *(3 marks)*

    i waxy layer _____

    _____

    ii spikes _____

    _____

    iii widespread roots _____

    _____

  b Organisms have developed adaptations to cope with seasonal changes. Describe **one** way a plant and **one** way an animal copes with the change from summer to winter. *(2 marks)*

    i Plant adaptation: _____

    _____

    ii Animal adaptation: _____

    _____

2 ⚗️⚗️ **Figure 1** is a food web which shows the feeding relationships between organisms living in a grass field.

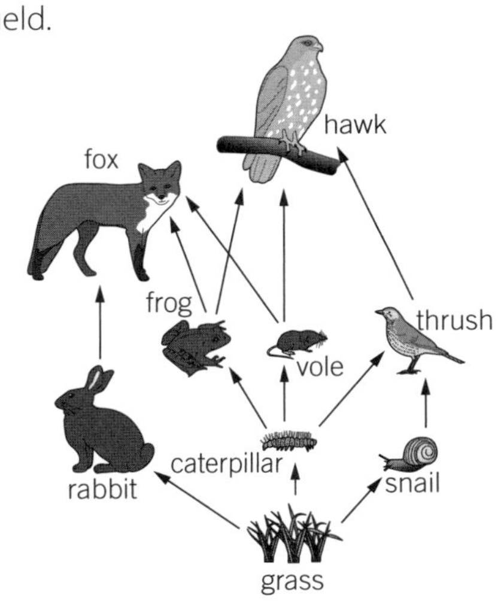

Figure 1

  a Describe what would happen to the rabbit population if the fox population was removed.

                                     (1 mark)

  _____

  b Describe what would happen to the vole population if the caterpillar population was removed. *(1 mark)*

  _____

  c An insecticide was sprayed to kill off the snail population. Chemicals from the insecticide remained in the body of the snails. Describe how this can result in the death of hawks. *(3 marks)*

  _____

  _____

  _____

  _____

3 ⚗️⚗️ A group of students were investigating the types of nutrient present in different ready meals.

  a Draw a line to match each nutrient to its role in the body. *(2 marks)*

Protein	Main source of energy
Lipids	To provide a store of energy and insulation, and protect organs
Carbohydrates	To repair body tissues and make new cells

  b The ready meals also contained fibre. Explain the importance of fibre in a person's diet. *(2 marks)*

  _____

  _____

  _____

  c One of the ready meals stated that it contained 2520 kJ of energy per pack. An average adult requires 8400 kJ of energy per day. Calculate the percentage of an adult's daily energy requirement contained within this pack. *(2 marks)*

  _____ kJ

d Describe how the students could prove that sugar was present in one of the ready meals. (*3 marks*)

_____

_____

_____

_____

4 Digestion begins in your mouth when food is chewed and mixed with saliva.

a i Name the enzyme present in saliva. (*1 mark*)

_____

ii Describe the role of this enzyme in digestion. (*2 marks*)

_____

_____

_____

b Explain why enzymes are called biological catalysts. (*2 marks*)

_____

_____

_____

c Bacteria that live in your large intestine play an important role in digestion. Describe the role these bacteria play. (*2 marks*)

_____

_____

_____

5 You get energy from the food you eat. This energy is transferred to your cells by respiration.

a i Complete the word equation for aerobic respiration. (*2 marks*)

glucose + _____ →

carbon dioxide + _____

ii Write down where in the cell respiration takes place. (*1 mark*)

_____

b Write down **two** differences between aerobic and anaerobic respiration in humans. (*2 marks*)

_____

_____

_____

_____

c i Write down what type of respiration is being represented by the following word equation:

glucose → ethanol + carbon dioxide (+ energy) (*1 mark*)

_____

ii Name an organism that performs this type of respiration. (*1 mark*)

_____

6 A group of Year 8 students studied variation within their class.

a Suggest one characteristic that they could investigate which shows:

i environmental variation (*1 mark*)

_____

ii inherited variation (*1 mark*)

_____

b The students also collected data on variation within holly leaves. Their data are shown in **Table 1**.

Table 1

Number of spikes	8	9	10	11	12
Frequency	8	10	15	12	14

i Plot the data using a bar chart on the graph paper below. (*4 marks*)

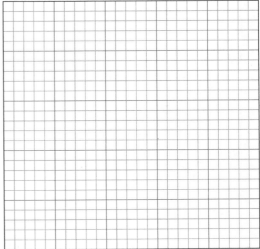

ii Give the most common number of spikes found on a holly leaf. (*1 mark*)

_____

c i Name the type of variation shown by this characteristic. (*1 mark*)

_____

ii Suggest how light could have caused this type of variation. (*3 marks*)

_____

_____

_____

_____

7 🜊🜊 Plants and animals compete for resources to survive. For example, plants compete for light.

a Describe one other resource that plants compete for. (*2 marks*)

_____

_____

b Explain why animals do not compete for light. (*2 marks*)

_____

_____

_____

c A new predator is introduced into an area. Describe how its prey species could change over a long period of time to survive a new predator. (*6 marks*)

_____

_____

_____

_____

_____

_____

_____

_____

8 🜊🜊🜊 Drugs are chemicals that affect the way the body works.

a Describe the difference between a recreational and a medical drug. (*2 marks*)

_____

_____

_____

b i Name the drug found in wine and beer. (*1 mark*)

_____

ii Give the long-term effects on the body of the drug identified in part **i**. (*3 marks*)

_____

_____

_____

_____

_____

c Smoking tobacco increases your risk of developing cardiovascular disease (CVD). This includes heart attacks and strokes.

i Explain how smoking can lead to heart disease. (*1 mark*)

_____

_____

_____

ii Study **Table 2**.

Table 2

Cigarettes smoked per day	CVD deaths per 100 000 men per year
0	572
1–14	802
15–24	892
25+	1025

Calculate the increase in the number of deaths due to CVD between men who smokes 20 cigarettes a day, compared to a non-smoker. (*1 mark*)

_____ per 100 000 men per year

iii Calculate the percentage of men dying from CVD each year who smoke 25 or more cigarettes per day. *(2 marks)*

_____ per 100 000 men per year

9 🧪🧪🧪 A group of students tested a variegated leaf for the presence of starch.

a Describe how to test a leaf for the presence of starch. *(3 marks)*

_____

_____

_____

_____

b i Shade in **Figure 2** below to show the results you would expect the students to see. *(1 mark)*

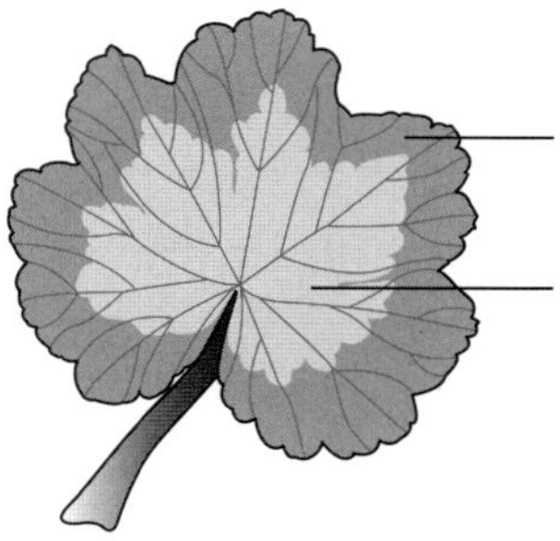

green part of leaf

white part of leaf

Figure 2

ii Explain your answer to part **i**. *(3 marks)*

_____

_____

_____

10 🧪🧪🧪 Chemosynthesis and photosynthesis are both types of chemical reaction.

a Describe **one** similarity and **one** difference between these chemical reactions. *(2 marks)*

_____

_____

_____

b i Name the organisms involved in a symbiotic relationship formed with chemosynthetic bacteria. *(1 mark)*

_____

ii Explain how this relationship benefits both organisms. *(2 marks)*

_____

_____

_____

11 🧪🧪🧪 A breeder of rabbits crossed a rabbit with brown spots with a rabbit with no spots.

a Explain why some of the rabbits had brown spots but some had no spots. *(1 mark)*

_____

_____

_____

b An adult rabbit has 44 chromosomes in its body cells. How many chromosomes are present in:

i a sperm cell? _____ *(1 mark)*

ii a fertilised egg cell? _____ *(1 mark)*

12 🧪🧪🧪 All organisms contain genetic material.

a Explain how genetic material is organised inside a cell. *(4 marks)*

_____

_____

_____

_____

b Explain how the structure of DNA was discovered. *(4 marks)*

_____

_____

_____

_____

B2 Checklist

Revision question number	Outcome	Topic reference	☹	😐	☺
1a	Describe how organisms are adapted to their environment.	B2 3.1			
1b	Describe how organisms adapt to environmental changes.	B2 3.2			
2a, b	Describe the interdependence of organisms.	B2 2.8			
2c	Describe how toxic materials can accumulate in a food web.	B2 2.8			
3a, b	Explain the role of each nutrient in the body.	B2 1.1			
3c	Calculate energy requirements.	B2 1.3			
3d	Describe how to test foods for the presence of sugars.	B2 1.2			
4a, b	Describe the role of enzymes in digestion.	B2 1.5			
4c	Describe the role of bacteria in digestion.	B2 1.5			
5a	State the word equation for aerobic respiration.	B2 2.5			
5b, c	Describe the differences between aerobic and anaerobic respiration.	B2 2.5			
6a	Describe the difference between environmental and inherited variation.	B2 3.3			
6bi	Represent variation within a species using graphs.	B2 3.4			
6bii	Describe the difference between continuous and discontinuous variation.	B2 3.4			
7a, b	Describe some resources that plants and animals compete for.	B2 3.1			
7c	Describe the process of natural selection.	B2 3.6			
8a	Describe the difference between medical and recreational drugs.	B2 1.6			
8b	Explain in detail how alcohol affects health and behaviour.	B2 1.7			
8c	Explain how smoking causes diseases Interpret secondary smoking data.	B2 1.8			
9a, b	Carry out an experiment to test a leaf for the presence of starch explaining the results obtained.	B2 2.1			
10a	Compare similarities and differences between photosynthesis and chemosynthesis.	B2 2.4			
10b	Explain how some chemosynthetic organisms form symbiotic relationships.	B2 2.4			
11a, b	Explain how characteristics are inherited.	B2 3.5			
12	Explain how scientists worked together to discover the structure of DNA.	B2 3.5			

C1.1 Metals and non-metals

A The elements are classified into metals and ____-_____. Metals are on the _____ of the stepped line in the Periodic Table, and non-metals are on the _____ of the stepped line. Most metals have _____ melting and boiling points. They are _____ conductors of heat and electricity. Metals make a ringing sound when you hit them – in other words, they are _____. The properties listed so far are properties that you can observe and measure, so they are _____ properties. Metals and non-metals also have different chemical reactions, so their _____ properties are different.

B The table shows the properties of four elements. Each element is represented by a letter. The letters are not the same as the chemical symbols for the elements.

Element	Melting point (°C)	Boiling point (°C)	Density (g/cm³)	Nature of the oxide of the element
J	714	1640	3.51	basic
K	−39	357	13.6	basic
L	44	280	1.82	acidic
M	113	445	2.07	acidic

a Write down the letters of the elements in the table that are metals. _____

b Explain how you decided whether element **J** is a metal or a non-metal.

_____

_____

C Germanium, Ge, is a metalloid element. It is used in solar cells and LED lights.

a Give the names and chemical symbols of two other metalloids.

_____ and _____

b Below is a list of some properties of germanium.

hard	semiconductor of electricity	melting point = 937 °C	shiny
brittle	density = 5.35 g/cm³	melting point of oxide = 1115 °C	

Compare the properties of germanium to the properties of a typical metal.

_____

_____

_____

_____

_____

_____

Hint: In your answer, describe how germanium is similar to a typical metal, and how germanium is different from a typical metal.

C1.2 Groups and periods

A In the Periodic Table, the vertical columns are called _____ and the horizontal rows are called

_____. There are patterns in the properties of the elements down _____ and across

_____. You can use patterns in the melting point of the elements in a _____ to predict

the melting point of an element whose melting point you do not know.

B The tables show the densities of some Group 3 and Group 4 elements.
Boron is at the top of Group 3 of the Periodic Table, and carbon is at the top of Group 4.

Group 3 element	Density (g/cm³)
boron	2.3
aluminium	2.7
gallium	5.9
indium	7.3
thallium	11.8

Group 4 element	Density (g/cm³)
carbon	2.2
silicon	2.3
germanium	5.3
tin	7.3
lead	

a A piece of lead has a volume of 5.0 cm³ and a mass of 56.5 g.

Calculate the density of lead. **Hint:** Use the equation: $density = \dfrac{mass}{volume}$

_____ g/cm³

b Compare the patterns in density for Group 3 and Group 4.

_____

_____

Hint: Describe the pattern in Group 3, then describe the pattern in Group 4. Then identify whether the patterns are similar or different.

C The tables below show data for elements in neighbouring groups in the Periodic Table.
Each table shows the elements in one group. The groups are arranged in the same order in the Periodic Table.

Period	Element	Melting point (°C)	Element	Melting point (°C)	Element	Melting point (°C)	Element	Melting point (°C)
4	Ti	1675	V	1900	Cr	1890	Mn	1240
5	Zr	1850	Nb	2470	Mo	2610	Tc	2200
6	Hf		Ta	3000	W	3410	Re	3180

a Compare the patterns in melting point for the Period 4 and Period 5 elements.

_____

_____

_____

b Suggest a value for the melting point of hafnium, and explain your prediction.

Melting point _____ °C

Reason _____

_____

_____

C1.3 The elements of Group 1

A Group 1 contains the elements in the column on the _____ of the Periodic Table. The Group 1 elements are metals. They _____ electricity and have _____ densities. The Group 1 elements react vigorously with water – in other words, they are very _____. When a Group 1 element reacts with water, _____ substances are made. These substances are _____ gas and a metal _____.

B The bar chart shows the melting and boiling points of the Group 1 elements.

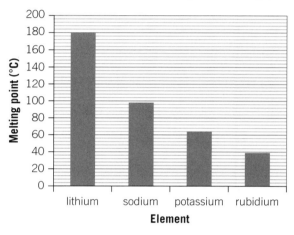 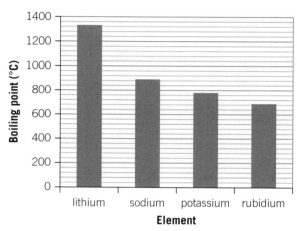

a Compare the patterns in melting point and boiling point for the Group 1 elements.

_____

_____

Hint: Look at the scales on the *y*-axis – they are different.

b Predict the melting point of caesium, which is below rubidium in Group 1.

_____ °C

C Dr Naylor heated three Group 1 elements in chlorine gas. The table shows what his students observed.

Group 1 element	Appearance during heating in chlorine gas	Appearance of product
lithium	burns well with red flame	white solid
sodium	burns strongly with bright orange flame	white solid
potassium	burns very strongly with lilac flame	white solid

a Predict the appearance of the product formed when rubidium is heated in chlorine gas.

_____

b The reaction between lithium and chlorine makes one product, lithium chloride.
Write a balanced symbol equation for the reaction.
Use these formulae: Li, Cl_2, LiCl

_____

c Predict the name of the product formed when caesium is heated in chlorine gas.

_____

C1.4 The elements of Group 7

A Group 7 contains the elements in the column that is second from the _____ of the Periodic Table.

The elements in Group 7 are also called the _____. They are non-_____. The Group 7

elements take part in displacement _____.

B A bottle of bromine has two hazard symbols.
Draw a line to match each hazard symbol to its meaning and risk. Then complete the empty boxes by writing one way of controlling each risk.

Hazard symbol	Meaning	Risk from this hazard	How to control the risk
	corrosive	difficulty breathing	
	toxic	burns eyes	

C A student mixes the solutions below. She does **not** mix the solutions shown by the shaded boxes.
The observations she makes are given in the list **V** to **Z** below.

Observations

V   pale green and colourless solutions react to make an orange solution ☐

W   orange and colourless solutions react to make a brown solution ☐

X   pale green and colourless solutions react to make a brown solution ☐

Y   no change observed ☐

Z   orange and colourless solutions react to make a green solution ☐

Complete the table by writing the letters of the correct observations for each reaction. You can use each letter once, more than once, or not at all.

	Potassium chloride solution	Potassium bromide solution	Potassium iodide solution
chlorine solution			
bromine solution			
iodine solution			

Hint: There is a displacement reaction when a more reactive element is mixed with a solution of a salt of a less reactive element. The Group 7 elements get **less** reactive from top to bottom of the group.

D **a**   Complete the table below.

Solutions that are mixed	✔ if a reaction occurs	Word equation (if the reaction occurs)
chlorine and potassium iodide		
fluorine and potassium chloride		
bromine and potassium fluoride		
iodine and potassium fluoride		

b   Explain how you made your predictions in the table.

_____

_____

C1.5 The elements of Group 0

A Group 0 contains the elements in the column on the _____ of the Periodic Table. The elements in Group 0 are also called the _____ gases. They are non-_____. Most Group 0 elements do not take part in chemical reactions – in other words, they are _____.

B a Draw one line from each element to show its chemical reactions.

Element

| **a** helium |

| **b** neon |

| **c** krypton |

| **d** xenon |

Chemical reactions

| **1** reacts with fluorine, the most reactive element |

| **2** reacts with oxygen and fluorine, which are very reactive |

| **3** none |

b Write a conclusion about the reactivity of the Group 0 elements and how this changes down the group.

_____

_____

C The table shows melting point data for the Group 0 elements.

a Describe the pattern in melting point for Group 0.

_____

b Predict the melting point of krypton, and explain how you made your prediction.

_____

_____

Element	Melting point (°C)
helium	−270
neon	−249
argon	−189
krypton	
xenon	−112

D The bar charts show the boiling points of the Group 1 and Group 0 elements.

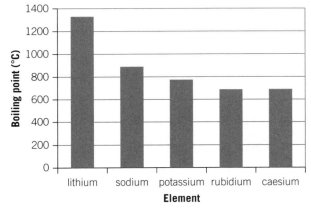

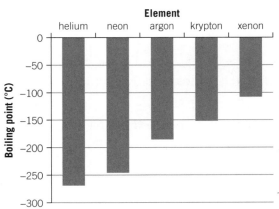

Compare the patterns in boiling points for the Group 1 and Group 0 elements.

_____

_____

_____

Pinchpoint question

Answer the question below, then do the follow-up activity **with the same letter** as the answer you picked.

This question is about the displacement reactions of the Group 7 elements. Which option below shows a displacement reaction that occurs **with** a correct explanation? You will need to use the Periodic Table in the back of this book.

A $Br_2 + 2KF \rightarrow 2KBr + F_2$
The reaction occurs because all Group 7 elements are very reactive.

B $Br_2 + 2KI \rightarrow 2KBr + I_2$
The reaction occurs because bromine is more reactive than iodine.

C $Br_2 + 2KCl \rightarrow 2KBr + Cl_2$
The reaction occurs because chlorine is more reactive than bromine.

D $Cl_2 + 2KF \rightarrow 2KCl + F_2$
The reaction occurs because chlorine is more reactive than the other elements in Group 7.

Follow-up activities

A In a displacement reaction, a more reactive Group 7 element pushes out a less reactive Group 7 element from its compound.

   a In each pair of elements below, underline the name of the **more** reactive Group 7 element.

      iodine and bromine   chlorine and iodine

      fluorine and chlorine   bromine and chlorine

   b **i** Look at the pairs of substances below. Underline the pairs where a displacement reaction will occur.

         iodine and potassium bromide   bromine and potassium iodide

         fluorine and potassium chloride   chlorine and potassium fluoride

         chlorine and potassium iodide   bromine and potassium chloride

     ii Write a word equation for each of the pairs that you underlined in part **i**.

_____

_____

_____

Hint: A displacement reaction occurs between a pair of substances if the **more** reactive Group 7 element is on its own, and if the **less** reactive Group 7 element is part of a compound. See C2 1.4 The elements of Group 7 for help.

B **a** Highlight or underline the **three** pairs of substances that react together in displacement reactions.

      fluorine and potassium chloride   chlorine and potassium iodide

      iodine and potassium fluoride   fluorine and potassium bromide

      iodine and potassium bromide   bromine and potassium fluoride

b Write balanced symbol equations for each of these three reactions.

_____

_____

_____

Hint: The chemical formulae of the elements and compounds you need for the equations are shown in the Pinchpoint question. See C2 1.4 The elements of Group 7 for help.

C Some of the sentences below include one or more mistakes.
Read the sentences and correct the mistakes.

A displacement reaction occurs between a pair of substances if the less reactive Group 7 element is on its own, and if the more reactive Group 7 element is part of a compound.

Fluorine is more reactive than chlorine. This means that fluorine and potassium chloride do not react together in a displacement reaction.

Iodine is more reactive than bromine. This means that potassium iodide and bromine react together in a decomposition reaction. The products are iodine and potassium bromine.

Hint: In a displacement reaction, a **more** reactive Group 7 element pushes out a **less** reactive Group 7 element from its compound. See C2 1.4 The elements of Group 7 for help.

D a List the elements in Group 7, from most reactive to least reactive.

_____

b Tick the true statements below.

1 Fluorine is more reactive than chlorine. ☐
2 There is no reaction between fluorine and potassium chloride. ☐
3 Iodine is more reactive than bromine. ☐
4 There is a displacement reaction between potassium iodide and bromine. ☐
5 Chlorine is more reactive than iodine. ☐
6 There is no reaction between potassium chloride and iodine. ☐
7 Fluorine is the most reactive element in Group 7. ☐
8 Fluorine displaces all the other Group 7 elements from their compounds with sodium. ☐

Hint: A displacement reaction occurs when a **more** reactive Group 7 element on its own displaces, or pushes out, a **less** reactive Group 7 element from its compound. See C2 1.4 The elements of Group 7 for help.

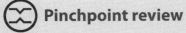

Pinchpoint review
Now look back at the question – do you think you chose the right letter?
Turn to the Answers page to find out.

C2.1 Mixtures

A If a substance does not have other substances mixed with it, it is _____ and has a _____ melting point. If a substance has other substances mixed with it, it is _____ and melts over a range of _____. A mixture contains _____ than one substance. Its different substances are _____ joined together. You can change the amounts of the different substances in a _____, and the substances in a mixture keep their own _____.

B A student measures the melting temperatures of four substances: **W**, **X**, **Y**, and **Z**. Her results are in the table.

Substance	Temperature the substance started to melt at (°C)	Temperature that the mixture finished melting at (°C)
W	11	13
X	51	51
Y	37	53
Z	79	79

Write down the letters of the **two** pure substances in the table, and explain how you decided.

Pure substances: _____ and _____

Reason for decision _____

C The diagrams below show some pure substances, and some mixtures, all in the gas state. Each circle represents one atom. Different colour circles represent atoms of different elements.

a Write down the letter of the correct diagram next to each description below.

   i A mixture of elements _____

   ii A pure element _____

   iii A pure compound _____

   iv A mixture of an element and a compound _____

b In the empty box, draw a diagram to show some particles in a mixture of two different compounds.

Hint: In a compound, each particle is made up of atoms of more than one element.

D Complete the table to describe how to separate each mixture, and why your chosen method works.

Mixture	How to separate the mixture	Why this method works
Sand and water		
Sand and steel nails		
Flour and marbles		

Hint: To help you to explain why each method works, think about the properties of the substances in the mixture.

C2.2 Solutions

A When you mix sugar with water, the sugar dissolves to make a _____. Sugar is the _____ and water is the _____. In a solution, several solvent particles surround each _____ particle. The particles _____ around. In a solution, you _____ see two separate substances, and all parts of the mixture are the _____. In a solution, the solvent is in the _____ state and the substance that dissolves in it can be in the solid or _____ state.

B For each pair of key words below, write one sentence about sugar and water. The sentence must include the two key words given, but none of the other key words.

For example: solvent, solution – In a solution of sugar in water, water is the solvent.

  a solvent, dissolves _____

  b solute, solvent _____

  c dissolves, solution _____

C **a** In the box, draw and label a diagram showing some sugar and water particles in sugar solution. Use different coloured circles to show the sugar and water particles. Sugar particles are bigger than water particles.

  b Describe what happens to the particles when sugar is added to water to make a solution.

  _____

D **a** Ophelia dissolves 12 g of paracetamol in 1000 g of water. What mass of solution does she make?

  _____

  b Marcus has 156 g of salt solution. He heats the solution and the water evaporates.
The mass of salt that remains is 7 g.
What mass of solvent was present in the original solution?

  _____

  c Normal saline solution is used in hospital drips. The solution usually contains 9.0 g of salt dissolved in 1004.6 g of solution.
Calculate the mass of water in 1004.6 g of the saline solution.

  _____

E **a** Nail polish remover is mainly propanone.
Suggest why propanone can remove nail polish, but water cannot.

  _____

  b A can of fizzy drink has four main ingredients – water, carbon dioxide, sugar, and flavourings.
Name the solvent and solutes in the drink.

  Solvent _____

  Solutes _____, _____, and _____

C2.3 Solubility

A A solution in which no more solute can dissolve is called a _____ solution. The mass of solute that

dissolves in 100 g of water to make a saturated solution is the _____ of the solute. If a substance

dissolves in a solvent, scientists say that the substance is _____. The greater the mass of solute that

can dissolve, the more _____ the solute.

B The sentences below are about solutions. There is one mistake in each sentence.
Copy out each sentence, correcting its mistake.

a A saturated sugar solution contains the minimum mass of sugar that will dissolve.

_____

b The solubility of sugar is the mass of sugar that dissolves in 100 g of water to make a dilute solution.

_____

c A saturated solution is one in which no more solvent will dissolve.

_____

C a The statements below can be reordered to describe an experiment to investigate the solubility of a solute at different temperatures. Read the statements and write down the order of statements you think will give the best method.

Correct order ☐ ☐ ☐ ☐ ☐

1   Heat up some water in a kettle, and repeat the whole experiment four more times at different temperatures.
2   Continue to add more and more solute to the water, with stirring, until no more dissolves.
3   At room temperature, weigh out 100 g of water in a beaker.
4   Use a spatula to add some solute to the water, and stir with a stirring rod.
5   Record the final mass of the solution.

b Describe how to calculate the mass of solute that dissolves in the experiment in part **a**.

_____

D The graph below shows the solubility of lead nitrate, and of potassium nitrate, at different temperatures.

a Draw a line of best fit on the graph for the solubility of lead nitrate.

b Tick the statements below that are true.

1   At all temperatures, lead nitrate is more soluble than potassium nitrate. ☐

2   At 80 °C, the mass of potassium nitrate that dissolves in 100 g of water is approximately 55 g more than the mass of lead nitrate that dissolves in 100 g of water. ☐

3   Lead nitrate is more soluble than potassium nitrate below 50 °C, but potassium nitrate is more soluble than lead nitrate above 50 °C. ☐

4   The solubility of lead nitrate is approximately 110 g/1000 g of water at 60 °C. ☐

C2.4 Filtration

A Filtration, also called _____, separates a liquid from an _____ solid. It can also separate excess solid that has not _____ in a solution. When you pour the mixture into filter paper, the _____ or solution goes through tiny holes in the filter paper. The liquid or solution is the _____. The solid remains in the filter paper cone. This is the _____.

B Label the diagram using the labels provided.

filter paper cone   filter funnel   conical flask   residue   filtrate   clamp

C The statements below can be reordered to explain how filtration works. Read the statements and write down the order of statements you think will give the best explanation.

Correct order ☐ ☐ ☐ ☐ ☐

1 so they stay in the filter paper.

2 Water particles are smaller than the tiny holes,

3 Filter paper has tiny holes in it.

4 Grains of sand are bigger than the tiny holes,

5 so they pass through the filter paper.

D a Tick the mixtures in the table that can be separated by filtration.
For the mixtures that can be separated, write down the names of the residue and filtrate.

	Mixture	✔ if separable by filtration	Residue	Filtrate
1	Pieces of dirt from oil in a car engine			
2	Undissolved potassium chloride from a saturated solution of potassium chloride			
3	Coffee solution from ground-up coffee beans			
4	Solid potassium chloride from a dilute solution of potassium chloride			

b Choose **one** mixture in the table above that **can** be separated by filtration.
Explain why this mixture can be separated by filtration.

_____

_____

E Look back at the solubility curve for potassium nitrate in C2.3.
A student makes a saturated solution by dissolving potassium nitrate in 100 g of water at 80 °C. She removes the undissolved potassium nitrate. Then the student cools the solution to 20 °C. She filters the mixture.
What is the maximum mass of solid potassium nitrate she can collect as residue?

maximum mass of solid potassium nitrate = _____ g

C2.5 Evaporation and distillation

A To obtain salt from salty water, you can use _____. The water evaporates, and salt (in the _____ state) remains. Evaporation is used to obtain any _____ from its solution. To obtain water from salty water, you need to use _____. Distillation uses evaporation and _____ to obtain a solvent from its _____.

B Mr Ward showed his class how to use distillation to obtain pure water from salty water. Add the labels below to the diagram to explain how distillation works.

1 Water vapour condenses here.   **2** Pure liquid water.

3 Water leaves the solution here, as a gas.   **4** The volume of this solution gets less.

5 This part of the apparatus is full of steam.

C Distillation and evaporation are both used to separate mixtures.

a Tick **one** or **two** boxes next to each statement to show whether the statement is true for distillation, evaporation, or both.

	Statement	✔ true for evaporation	✔ true for distillation
1	The solvent changes state from liquid to gas.		
2	The purpose of the technique is to obtain a substance in the solid state.		
3	The solute remains in the container that is heated.		
4	The solvent evaporates, condenses, and is collected.		
5	The solvent vapour is not usually collected.		

b Write two sentences to compare distillation and evaporation.

_____

_____

_____

Hint: In your answer, write one sentence about how the processes are similar, and one sentence about how the processes are different.

D Jasmine has some copper chloride solution. The solvent in the solution is water.

a Name the one substance that Jasmine can obtain from this solution by distillation.

_____

b Explain why Jasmine can use distillation, but not evaporation, to obtain this substance from the solution.

_____

_____

_____

C2.6 Chromatography

A The dyes that are mixed together in ink are soluble in the same _____. This means that you can separate them by _____. In this process, the different dyes travel _____ distances up the paper. This separates the dyes, which each make a separate _____ on the chromatogram.

B Sam ground up some leaves with a solvent, and put a spot of the juice on a piece of chromatography paper. On the same paper, he also put spots of three other pigments (colours) that he thought might be in the leaves. These are his reference spots.

Here is Sam's chromatogram.

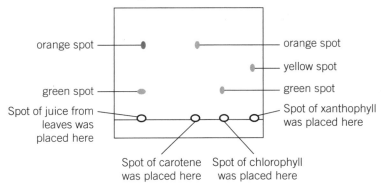

a How many pigments are in the leaves? _____

b Name the two pigments that are probably in the leaves.

_____ and _____

c Explain why you cannot be certain that the pigments you named in part **b** are in the leaves.

_____

d Name one pigment that is **not** in Sam's leaves.

_____

C Zoe wants to use chromatography to determine whether two reactants have finished reacting.

She starts by making a reference chromatogram. She carries out a chromatography experiment with the two reactants and the product of the chemical reaction (chromatogram **A**).

She then carries out the chemical reaction. After a few minutes she takes out a small sample of the reaction mixture, and makes chromatogram **B**.

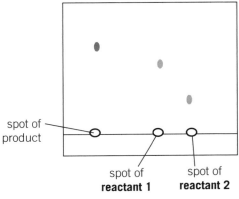

Chromatogram **A**

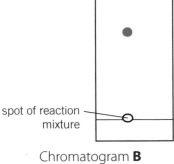

Chromatogram **B**

Use information from both chromatograms to explain whether or not the reactants have finished reacting.

_____

_____

Pinchpoint question

Answer the question below, then do the follow-up activity **with the same letter** as the answer you picked.

The graph shows the solubility of ammonium chloride at different temperatures.

Hassan dissolves ammonium chloride in 100 g of water at 80 °C to make a saturated solution. He removes the undissolved solid.

Hassan then cools his solution to 20 °C, and some solid comes out of solution.

At 20 °C, Hassan filters the mixture. What is the mass of solid in the filter paper?

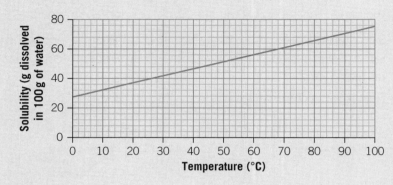

A 66 g   **B** 56 g

C 37 g   **D** 29 g

Follow-up activities

A Tick the true statements below.

1   You can use filtration to separate a liquid from a solid that does not dissolve in it.   ☐

2   You can use filtration to separate all the solute that is dissolved in a solution.   ☐

3   You can use filtration to separate undissolved solid from its saturated solution.   ☐

4   You can use filtration to separate some, but not all, of the solute that is dissolved in a solution.   ☐

5   If you filter a mixture of 65 g of sand and 100 g of water, there will be 65 g of sand in the filter paper. ☐

6   If you filter a mixture of 122 g of saturated sugar solution and 11 g of undissolved sugar, there will
    be 133 g of sugar in the filter paper.   ☐

Hint: When you filter a mixture of a saturated solution and its undissolved solid, only the undissolved solid will end up in the filter paper. See C2 2.3 Solubility and C2 2.4 Filtration for help.

B When you cool a saturated solution of ammonium chloride, some ammonium chloride will come out of solution. Complete the tables below. You will need to select data from the graph.
The first row of each table has been done for you.

Temperature (°C)	Solubility (g dissolved in 100 g of water)
0	28
10	
40	
60	
90	

Temperature change (°C)	Mass of solute that comes out of solution when this temperature change occurs (g)
from 90 to 60	70 − 56 = 14
from 60 to 0	
from 40 to 10	
from 90 to 10	
from 30 to 20	

Hint: Use data from the first table to help you to complete the second table (except for the final row). See C2 2.3 Solubility for help.

C Draw a line from each sentence starter to its correct ending. Use each ending once, more than once, or not at all. You will need to select data from the graph.

a The graph shows that the solubility of ammonium chloride	**1** 61 g.
b At 70 °C, the mass of ammonium chloride that dissolves in 100 g of water is	**2** increases as temperature increases.
c At 40 °C, the mass of ammonium chloride that dissolves in 100 g of water is	**3** 61 g – 46 g = 15 g.
d When you cool ammonium chloride from 70 °C to 40 °C, the mass of ammonium chloride that comes out of solution is	**4** 46 g.
e When you filter a saturated solution of ammonium chloride that was made at 70 °C and cooled to 40 °C, the mass of solid in the filter paper is	**5** decreases as temperature increases.

Hint: For most substances, when you cool their saturated solution, some solid comes out of the solution. See C2 2.3 Solubility for help.

D Work out the answers to the questions below. You will need to select data from the graph.

a Alex has 200 g of water. What mass of ammonium chloride dissolves in the water to make a saturated solution at 50 °C?

b Samuel has 100 g of water at 40 °C. He adds ammonium chloride to make a saturated solution. What is the mass of the solution?

c Lola has 100 g of water at 90 °C. She makes a saturated solution of ammonium chloride, and removes the undissolved solid. Then she cools the solution to 0 °C and filters the mixture. What mass of solid is in the filter paper?

d Alishba has 100 g of water at 70 °C. She makes a saturated solution of ammonium chloride, and removes the undissolved solid. Then she cools the solution and filters the mixture. She collects 19 g of solid in the filter paper. To what temperature did she cool the solution?

Hint: The mass of a solution is equal to the total mass of the solvent and solute. See C2 2.3 Solubility and C2 2.4 Filtration for help.

Pinchpoint review

Now look back at the question – do you think you chose the right letter?
Turn to the Answers page to find out.

C3.1 Acids and metals

A Most elements are _____. They have similar physical properties; for example, they are shiny, and they conduct heat and _____. Metals also have patterns in their chemical properties. For example, some metals react with dilute acids to make salts and _____ gas. Magnesium reacts with dilute hydrochloric acid to make _____ chloride and hydrogen.

B **a** Complete the results table for the experiment.

Metal	Observations
magnesium	
zinc	
iron	
lead	A few bubbles formed, very slowly.

magnesium   zinc   iron   lead

b Write a conclusion for Magda's experiment. In your conclusion, include the words in the box.

reactive	hydrogen	vigorous

_____

_____

C Magda collects the gas in the bubbles in the experiment in activity **B**.
She wants to check that the gas is hydrogen.

a Describe how to test for hydrogen gas. In your answer, write down how Magda will know if the gas is hydrogen.

_____

_____

_____

b This test is the reaction of hydrogen with oxygen. Complete the written equation for this test reaction.

hydrogen + _____ → _____

c Balance the symbol equation for the reaction of hydrogen with oxygen.

_____$H_2 + O_2 \rightarrow$ _____H_2O

Hint: Do not change the chemical formulae; just put numbers on the left of the formulae, as needed.

D If a metal reacts with dilute hydrochloric acid, the products are hydrogen and a solution of a metal chloride. If a metal reacts with sulfuric acid, the products are hydrogen and a metal sulfate solution.

Complete and balance the equations below.

a $Mg + H_2SO_4 \rightarrow MgSO_4 +$ _____

b _____ + _____$HCl \rightarrow MgCl_2 + H_2$

c $Zn +$ _____ $\rightarrow ZnSO_4 +$ _____

d $Zn +$ _____$HCl \rightarrow$ _____$Cl_2 +$ _____

C3.2 Metals and oxygen

A Some metals react with oxygen from the _____. The more _____ the metal, the more vigorous the reaction. For example, magnesium burns vigorously to make magnesium _____.

Copper does not burn when you heat it in a Bunsen burner flame. Instead, it forms a layer of black copper _____ on its surface. Gold does not react with oxygen. It is an _____ metal.

State symbols in equations show the _____ of a substance in the reaction. The state symbol for _____ is (s) and the state symbol for _____ is (l).

B Zion heats small pieces of five metals in a Bunsen burner flame.
She writes her observations in the table below.

Metal	Observations when heated in a Bunsen burner flame
copper	Does not burn. Forms layer of black copper oxide on its surface
iron	Small pieces burn, but less vigorously than zinc
gold	No change in appearance
magnesium	Burns vigorously
zinc	Small pieces burn, but less vigorously than magnesium

Write a conclusion for Zion's experiment. In your conclusion, use the words in the box.

reactive	unreactive	vigorously	magnesium oxide	copper oxide

_____

_____

_____

_____

_____

C **a** Use the observations in the table in activity **B** to write the names of the metals in order of reactivity, with the most reactive at the top. Two have been done for you.

magnesium

_____

_____

_____

gold

b Explain the order of reactivity you chose in part **a**.

_____

_____

D Complete and balance the equations below. Include state symbols.

a ___$Cu(s) + O_2(\_\_) \rightarrow$ ___$CuO(s)$

b 2___$(s) + O_2(g) \rightarrow$ ___$MgO(\_\_)$

c ___$Zn(s) +$ ___$(g) \rightarrow$ ___$ZnO(s)$

d ___$Fe(\_\_) +$ ___$O_2(\_\_) \rightarrow$ ___$Fe_2O_3(\_\_)$

C3.3 Metals and water

A The reactivity series lists the _____ in order of how vigorously they react. The metals at the _____ of the reactivity series react vigorously with water, oxygen, and dilute acids. The metals at the bottom of the reactivity series are _____. Metals that react with water include potassium, sodium, lithium, and calcium. The products of their reactions are _____ gas and the metal _____.

Part of the reactivity series
rubidium
lithium
calcium
magnesium
aluminium
zinc
iron
lead
copper
silver
gold

B Magnesium and potassium react with water. The diagrams show their reactions.

a Complete the table to compare the reactions of potassium and magnesium.

Metal	How vigorous is the reaction?	Name of the product that is formed in the gas state	Name of the other product
magnesium			
potassium			

b Write a paragraph, based on the information in the table, to compare the reactions of magnesium and potassium with water.

_____

_____

_____

_____

C Sarah has samples of three metals – calcium, magnesium, and silver. She does not know which metal is which.

a Describe a simple investigation Sarah could do to find out which metal is which. In your answer name **two** variables that Sarah must control to make sure that the investigation is fair.

_____

_____

_____

b Explain how Sarah could use her results to decide which metal is which.

_____

_____

_____

Hint: Use the reactivity series on this page to help you.

C3.4 Metal displacement reactions

A Metals take part in displacement reactions. In a displacement reaction, a _____ reactive metal pushes out a _____ reactive metal from its compound. For example, in the thermite reaction, aluminium displaces iron from _____ _____. The products of the reaction are aluminium _____ and _____.

B The equation shows a displacement reaction.

$Mg(s) + CuSO_4(aq) \rightarrow MgSO_4(aq) + Cu(s)$

The statements below are about the reaction in the equation. There is one mistake in each statement. Use a coloured pen to correct each mistake.

a Magnesium is below copper in the reactivity series.

b Magnesium is less reactive than copper.

c Magnesium displaces copper from its compound, copper chloride.

d As the reaction takes place, the colour of the blue copper sulfate solution gets darker.

e As the reaction takes place, the piece of magnesium gets bigger.

C Draw a tick next to each pair of substances that you predict will react together.

Then use the reactivity series in C3.3 to explain your prediction for each of the three pairs of substances.

	Pair of substances	✔ if a reaction occurs	Scientific explanation of prediction
1	copper and magnesium chloride solution		
2	magnesium and lead oxide		
3	zinc and lead nitrate		

D The particle diagram below represents the displacement reaction of magnesium with copper oxide.

_____   _____   _____

a Label the diagram with the labels in the box.

magnesium atom   **copper atom**   **oxygen atom**

b Explain what the diagram shows.

_____

E Use ideas about the reactivity series to explain the observations below.

a Mike adds some small pieces of zinc to copper sulfate solution. A pink-brown solid forms, and the colour of the blue solution becomes paler.

_____

_____

b Bridie heats a mixture of iron and aluminium oxide powder. There is no reaction.

_____

_____

C3.5 Extracting metals

A Most metals exist in the Earth's _____ as compounds. These compounds are _____ with other compounds in rock. A rock that it is worth extracting a metal from is called an _____. Many metals are extracted from their compounds in _____ reactions. For example, iron oxide is heated with carbon. The carbon _____ iron from iron oxide. The products of the reaction are _____ and carbon dioxide.

B An ore is a rock that it is worth extracting a metal from.
The statements below can be reordered to describe how to get iron from iron ore.
Read the statements and write down the order of statements you think will give the best description.

Correct order ☐ ☐ ☐

1 Separate iron oxide from compounds that are mixed with it.

2 Dig the iron ore out of the ground.

3 Use a displacement reaction to extract iron from iron oxide.

C Draw a tick next to each metal that you predict can be extracted by heating with carbon. Then use the reactivity series on this page, and the idea of displacement, to explain each prediction.

Metal	✔ if can be extracted by heating with carbon	Scientific explanation of prediction
zinc		
magnesium		
lead		

Part of the reactivity series (including carbon, a non-metal)

calcium
magnesium
aluminium
carbon
zinc
iron
lead
copper

D a A zinc mine in India supplies zinc ore that is 41% zinc.
Calculate the mass of zinc in 500 kg of the ore.

_____

b A 5 kg sample of lead ore from a mine in China contains 200 g of lead.
Calculate the percentage of lead in the ore.

_____

Hint: Before you start this calculation, convert the mass of the sample to grams.

E There are several ores of lead. Two of them are lead sulfide, PbS, and lead carbonate, $PbCO_3$.
For each of the following, write a word equation and a balanced symbol equation for the reaction.

Formulae: Pb, PbS, PbO, SO_2, O_2, $PbCO_3$, PbO, CO_2, C

a The first step in extracting lead from lead sulfide is to heat the compound in air. The lead sulfide reacts with oxygen to make lead oxide and sulfur dioxide.
Word equation _____
Balanced symbol equation _____

b The first step in extracting lead from lead carbonate is to heat the compound, which decomposes to make lead oxide and carbon dioxide.
Word equation _____
Balanced symbol equation _____

c Lead oxide (obtained from both lead sulfide and lead carbonate) is heated with carbon. A displacement reaction occurs. The products are lead oxide and carbon dioxide.
Word equation _____
Balanced symbol equation _____

C3.6 Ceramics

A Ceramics are compounds. They include metal silicates, _____ oxides, and _____ carbides. Ceramics are hard, stiff, and brittle. They have very _____ melting points and are electrical _____. These are _____ properties. Ceramics also have similar chemical properties to each other – they do not react with water, acids, or _____.

B Draw **one** line to match each property to the statement that **best** explains why a ceramic material has this property.

Property	Best explanation of property
a Very hard	**1** Does not have charged particles that can move.
b Does not conduct electricity	**2** Needs a large amount of energy to break bonds between atoms.
c High melting point	**3** The bonds between the particles are very strong.

C The table lists some properties of ceramics.
Draw **one** tick next to each property to show whether the property is a chemical property or a physical property.

	Property	✔ if a chemical property	✔ if a physical property
1	Brittle – break easily and cannot be moulded easily		
2	Do not react with water		
3	Do not conduct electricity		
4	Stiff – difficult to bend		

Hint: Chemical properties describe how a substance behaves in its chemical reactions.

D For each use of a ceramic material below, write down **two** properties that make ceramics suitable for this use.

a Making insulators for electrical power lines

_____

_____

b Making jet engine blades, which get very hot

_____

_____

E Ruby sets up the apparatus below to compare the strengths of different ceramic materials. She finds the mass that makes the piece of ceramic break.

Complete the sentences below.

a The independent variable is _____

b Two of the control variables are _____

c The purpose of the clamp, boss and clamp stand is _____

_____

d 100 g masses are used instead of 1 kg masses because _____

_____

ceramic material

masses

C3.7 Polymers

A A polymer is a substance with very _____ molecules. Its molecules have identical groups of atoms, repeated _____ times. There are _____ polymers, each with _____ properties. The properties of polymers depend on the groups of _____ in their molecules.

B The table shows data for some polymers.

Polymer	Strength when pulled (MPa)	Density (g/cm³)	Flexibility	Is it waterproof?
LDPE	15	0.92	very flexible	yes
HDPE	15	0.96	rigid	yes
Poly(propene)	40	0.90	very flexible	yes
flexible PVC	20	1.30	very flexible	yes
rigid PVC	60	1.30	rigid	yes
nylon 6	70	1.13	very flexible	yes

a Poly(propene) is used to make ropes for ships. Use data from the table to explain why it is suitable for this use.

_____

b Catherine says that it would be better to make ropes from nylon 6 than from poly(propene). Choose data from the table to suggest why.

_____

c Choose two polymers that are suitable for making water bottles. Give reasons for your choices.

Polymers: _____ and _____

Reasons: _____

d Compare the properties of LDPE and flexible PVC.

_____

_____

_____

Hint: Write about how the two polymers are similar, and how they are different. Include data from the table in your answer.

C The diagrams show the molecules in two different polymers.

Suggest why polymer **X** is flexible and polymer **Y** is rigid.

polymer **X**   polymer **Y**

_____

_____

_____

D Outdoor chairs can be made of wood or synthetic polymers such as high-density poly(ethene), HDPE. Use information from the table, and your own knowledge, to compare the advantages and disadvantages of the two materials.

_____

_____

_____

_____

C3.8 Composites

A A composite material is a _____ of materials. The different materials have _____ properties. The properties of the composite are a _____ of these properties. For example, reinforced concrete is a composite material. It contains steel and concrete. Steel is not damaged by stretching forces, and concrete is not damaged by _____ forces. This means that reinforced concrete is not damaged by either stretching or _____ forces.

B Tick the statements below that are true.

1 A composite material is a compound of materials. ☐

2 A composite has properties that are a combination of the properties of the materials it is made up of. ☐

3 Reinforced concrete is stronger than concrete if you hang weights from it. ☐

C **a** A car tyre is a composite material, made from steel cords covered in rubber.

i Describe what a composite material is.

_____

_____

ii Suggest one advantage of including steel cords in a car tyre, compared to making a tyre of rubber only.

_____

b A tall building is made of reinforced concrete, which consists of steel rods surrounded by concrete. Explain why it is better to use reinforced concrete rather than concrete alone.

_____

_____

_____

_____

D The table shows some properties of steel and carbon-fibre-reinforced plastic, CFRP.

Material	Density (g/cm³)	Strength when pulled (MPa)	Does the material rust?
Steel	8.0	300	yes
CFRP	1.8	1450	no

Colin is buying a bicycle. He tests a bicycle made from CFRP that costs £1000, and a bicycle made from steel that costs £200. Use data from the table to explain why it might be worth paying more for the CFRP bicycle.

_____

_____

_____

_____

_____

C2 Chapter 3 Pinchpoint

Pinchpoint question

Answer the question below, then do the follow-up activity **with the same letter** as the answer you picked.

Which metals can be extracted by heating their naturally occurring compounds with carbon, and why?

Use the reactivity series to help you.

A Chromium and nickel, because they are less reactive than carbon.

B Beryllium and chromium, because their reactivities are similar to the reactivity of carbon.

C Rubidium and beryllium, because they are less reactive than carbon.

D Barium and strontium, because they are more reactive than carbon.

Reactivity series	
rubidium	**most reactive**
potassium	
barium	
strontium	
beryllium	
carbon	
chromium	
nickel	
copper	**least reactive**

Follow-up activities

A A metal that is less reactive than carbon may be extracted from its compound by heating the compound with carbon. Carbon displaces the metal from its compound. Some metals are extracted from their compounds in displacement reactions with elements other than carbon.

The displacement reactions below are all used to extract metals from their compounds.
For each displacement reaction, circle the name of the **more** reactive metal (or non-metal) in the word equation. Then balance the symbol equation.

a titanium chloride + sodium → titanium + sodium chloride

$$TiCl_4 + \underline{\quad}Na \rightarrow Ti + \underline{\quad}NaCl$$

b chromium oxide + aluminium → aluminium oxide + chromium

$$Cr_2O_3 + \underline{\quad}Al \rightarrow Al_2O_3 + \underline{\quad}Cr$$

c tungsten oxide + hydrogen → tungsten + water

$$WO_3 + \underline{\quad}H_2 \rightarrow W + \underline{\quad}H_2O$$

Hint: When balancing a chemical equation, do not change any of the chemical formulae. See C2 3.3 Metals and water, C2 3.4 Metal displacement reactions, and C2 3.5 Extracting metals for help.

B Draw one line from each sentence starter to its correct ending. Use each ending once, more than once, or not at all. You will need to refer to the reactivity series above.

1	because it is a metal.

a In the reactivity series, metals are listed in order of

2	increasing reactivity from top to bottom.

b Carbon can be included in the reactivity series

3	the metal is less reactive than carbon.

c Carbon may displace a metal from its compounds if

4	decreasing reactivity from top to bottom.

d Carbon may not be used to extract strontium from its compounds because

5	even though it is not a metal.

6	the metal is more reactive than carbon.

Hint: Which is more reactive, potassium or copper? Where are these metals in the reactivity series on the page opposite? What does this tell you about the order of metals in the reactivity series? See C2 3.3 Metals and water, C2 3.4 Metal displacement reactions, and C2 3.5 Extracting metals for help.

C If a metal is **less** reactive than carbon, it may be extracted from its compound by heating the compound with carbon. The reactivity series lists metals in order of their reactivity.

In each list below, use a pen to draw a circle around the **most** reactive metal and use a pencil to draw a circle around the **least** reactive metal. Use the reactivity series on the page opposite to help you.

a	rubidium	nickel	strontium
b	chromium	barium	potassium
c	copper	beryllium	barium
d	potassium	rubidium	strontium
e	copper	nickel	chromium

Hint: Copper is the least reactive metal in the reactivity series shown on the opposite page. What does this tell you about the order of metals in the reactivity series? See C2 3.3 Metals and water for help.

D Some of the sentences and word equations below include one or more mistakes. Read the sentences and correct the mistakes.

The reactivity series lists metals in order of reactivity. Metals at the bottom are more reactive than metals at the top.

Carbon is also included in the reactivity series, even though it is not a metal.

If a metal is above carbon in the reactivity series, it is less reactive than carbon.

A metal that is more reactive than carbon may be extracted from its compounds by heating with carbon. A decomposition reaction occurs.

The word equations below show examples of displacement reactions in which a metal is extracted from a compound by heating with hydrogen:

tin oxide + carbon → tin oxide + carbon dioxide

lead oxide + carbon dioxide → lead + carbon dioxide

Hint: Copper can be extracted from its compounds by heating with carbon. What does this tell you about the position in the reactivity series of metals that can be extracted by heating with carbon? See C2 3.3 Metals and water, C2 3.4 Metal displacement reactions, and C2 3.5 Extracting metals for help.

 Pinchpoint review
Now look back at the question – do you think you chose the right letter?
Turn to the Answers page to find out.

A The Earth is made up of four _____. In the centre is the solid _____ core, which is surrounded by the liquid _____ core. Outside the outer core is the _____. This is mainly _____ rock, but it can _____. On the surface of the Earth is the rocky _____, which is between 8 km and 40 km thick. The gases of the _____ surround the Earth. The layer of the atmosphere nearest the Earth is the _____. This is a mixture of gases, including 78% _____ and 21% _____.

B Write **three** sentences to compare the properties of the different layers of the Earth.

_____

_____

_____

C a Nitrogen makes up 78% of the air.

Calculate the volume of nitrogen in a classroom of volume 250 m³.

_____ m³

b A 400 m³ sample of air contains 84 m³ of gas X.

i Calculate the percentage of the air that is gas X.

_____ %

ii Suggest the name of gas X, and give a reason for your suggestion.

_____

D You can use a hard-boiled egg in its shell to model the structure of the Earth.

shell
white
yolk

a Give **two** ways in which the egg is similar to the structure of the Earth.

_____

_____

b Describe **two** ways in which the egg is not a good model for the structure of the Earth.

_____

_____

Hint: In your answer, write down how the model and the structure of the Earth are similar. Then write down how they are different.

C4.2 Sedimentary rocks

A There are three types of rock – igneous, sedimentary, and _____. Most types of sedimentary rock

are porous and _____ . Sedimentary rocks are formed when rock breaks up into smaller pieces by

physical, chemical, or _____ weathering. The smaller pieces, called _____, move away

from the rock and are carried far away by _____ processes. The sediments settle in one place. This is

_____. Then the sediments join together by _____ or _____.

In _____, the weight of the sediments above _____ together the sediments below. In

_____, another substance sticks the sediments together.

B The statements below can be reordered to describe how sedimentary rocks are made. Read the statements and
write down the order of statements you think will give the best description. Start with statement number 1.

Correct order ☐ ☐ ☐ ☐

1 Weathering breaks up all types of rock into much smaller pieces or sediments.

2 The sediments stop moving and settle in one place in a process called deposition.

3 The sediments join together to make new rock.

4 These small sediments are transported far away from the rock.

C This question is about the formation of sedimentary rocks.

a Name **three** types of weathering, and write down a definition for each type.

_____

_____

_____

_____

_____

_____

_____

b Explain what is meant by the phrase **transport of sediments**.

_____

D Complete the table to explain each property of a typical sedimentary rock.

In your answers, refer to the structure of the rock, and how it was formed.

Property	Reason for property in terms of the structure of the rock and how it was formed
Porous	
Soft	

C4.3 Igneous and metamorphic rocks

A Underground, liquid rock is called _____. On the surface, liquid rock is called _____.

Igneous rocks form when liquid rock cools and _____. They are made up of _____,

which are joined together with no gaps. This means that igneous rocks are _____-_____. They are also

durable and _____. Metamorphic rocks form when heat and/or high _____ change

existing rock. Metamorphic rocks are made up of _____, so they are non-porous.

B a Describe one similarity between igneous and metamorphic rocks.

_____

b Describe one difference in the way that igneous and metamorphic rocks are formed.

_____

_____

C Salol is a compound that has a melting point of 42 °C. When hot liquid salol cools down in the lab, it freezes to make crystals. Maddie has some liquid salol. She places a few drops on a cold microscope slide, and a few drops on a warm microscope slide. She obtains the results shown below.

a Complete the table below to describe and explain the observations from Maddie's experiment.

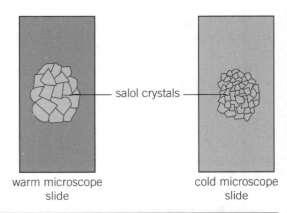

warm microscope slide   cold microscope slide

Relative temperature of microscope slide	Observations	Explanation of observations
warm		
cold		

b Use information from the table you completed in part **a** to explain why igneous rock formed underground has bigger crystals than igneous rock formed on the surface.

_____

_____

_____

D Complete the table to explain each property of a typical igneous rock. In your answers, refer to the structure of the rock, and how it was formed.

Property	Reason for property in terms of the structure of the rock
Not porous	
Hard	

C4.4 The rock cycle

A The rock cycle shows how the materials in rocks are _____. For example, when a rock of any type

is weathered, its sediments may form _____ rocks. When a rock melts, the liquid rock later cools

and _____ to make an _____ rock. When a rock experiences high pressures or

_____, its particles may be rearranged, forming a _____ rock. When forces from inside

the Earth push rocks upwards, _____ occurs.

B Each number below represents a process that helps to convert rock from one type to another.

    1 cooling

    2 freezing

    3 melting

    4 the action of heat

    5 the action of high pressure

    6 weathering

    7 transport

    8 deposition

    9 cementation

    10 compaction

Label the diagram of the rock cycle by writing **one or more** numbers in each box. Use each number as many times
as you need to.

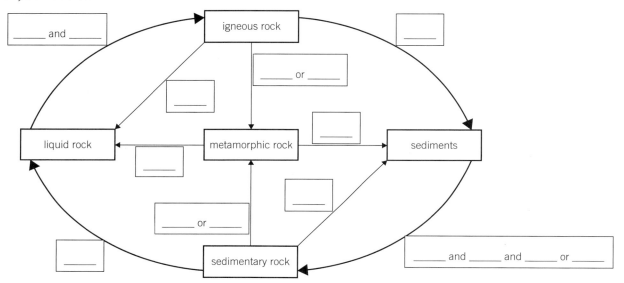

C Write a paragraph to describe one possible journey of some material around the rock cycle.

In your answer, include at least three steps.

For example, you might like to start with plant roots growing in a crack in the rock, and small pieces breaking off the
rock. What might happen next?

There are many possible answers to this question.

_____

_____

_____

_____

_____

_____

C4.5 The carbon cycle

A There are several carbon stores, or _____. These include the atmosphere, the ocean,

_____ rocks, _____ fuels, plants and animals, and the soil. The carbon

_____ shows how carbon atoms move between stores. For example, carbon dioxide enters the

atmosphere when plants and animals _____. It also enters the atmosphere when fossil fuels

_____. Carbon dioxide leaves the atmosphere when plants use it in _____. It also

leaves the atmosphere by _____ in oceans. Before industrialisation, carbon dioxide was added to the

atmosphere at the _____ rate as it left the atmosphere. This meant that the concentration of carbon

dioxide did not _____.

B The diagram below shows the carbon cycle.

In each box, write the name of the correct carbon store (also called a carbon reservoir).

Along each arrow, write the name of the correct **one** or **two** processes from the box below.

combustion	**respiration**	**decay without oxygen**	**photosynthesis**
dissolving	**rock formation**	**coming out of solution**	

C Use the carbon cycle to help you to complete the sentences below.

a For many years, the concentration of carbon dioxide in the atmosphere remained constant because

_____

_____

_____

b Since industrialisation, the concentration of carbon dioxide in the atmosphere has increased because

_____

_____

_____

C4.6 Climate change

A Since 1800, _____ carbon dioxide has been added to the atmosphere than has been removed. This is partly because humans burn _____ fuels. It is also because humans cut down lots of trees. This is _____ . Carbon dioxide in the atmosphere absorbs some of the solar _____ reflected off the Earth's surface. This keeps the Earth _____ than it would otherwise be. This is called the _____ _____ . Extra carbon dioxide results in _____ average global temperatures, which is _____ _____ . This causes _____ change, leading to rising sea levels and more extreme _____ events.

B Draw a line to match each cause to one direct effect.

Cause	Effect
a Deforestation	**1** More carbon dioxide goes into the atmosphere
b Burning fossil fuels	**2** The concentration of carbon dioxide in the atmosphere increases
c Every year, more carbon dioxide is added to the atmosphere than is removed	**3** Less carbon dioxide is removed from the atmosphere
d Climate change	**4** Rising sea levels, floods, and more hurricanes and droughts

C The statements below can be reordered to explain how climate change occurs. Read the statements and write down the order of statements that gives the best explanation.

Correct order: ☐ ☐ ☐ ☐ ☐ ☐ ☐

1 The Sun emits radiation, which reaches the Earth.

2 This extra carbon dioxide in the atmosphere means that more of the radiation that is reflected from the surface is absorbed by the atmosphere. This warms the atmosphere by a greater amount than before.

3 Some of this radiation is absorbed by gases in the atmosphere, such as carbon dioxide.

4 Human activities add extra carbon dioxide to the atmosphere.

5 This causes global warming, which is an increase in global average temperatures. Global warming results in climate change.

6 Some of the radiation from the Sun is absorbed by the Earth. The rest of the radiation is reflected by the surface.

7 This is a long-term change in weather patterns.

D Explain **six** impacts of climate change.

In your answer, include **three pairs** of impacts. Each pair should include one primary impact and a related secondary impact.

_____

_____

_____

_____

_____

_____

C4.7 Recycling

A Recycling means collecting and _____ used materials so that they can be used again. There are

many advantages of recycling, including _____ energy needs. Disadvantages of recycling include

the _____ produced by lorries that collect objects for recycling.

B The statements below can be reordered to describe how aluminium is recycled. Read the statements and write
down the order of statements you think will give the best description.

Correct order: ☐ ☐ ☐ ☐ ☐ ☐

1   Use a lorry to collect used cans.
2   Pour the liquid aluminium into a mould.
3   Leave the liquid aluminium to cool and freeze.
4   Melt the shreds of aluminium in a furnace.
5   Shred the cans.
6   Use magnets to separate aluminium cans from steel cans.

C Evaluate the advantages and disadvantages of recycling aluminium compared to extracting the metal from its ore.

Hint: Start by giving some advantages and disadvantages of recycling aluminium compared to extracting the
metal from its ore. Then discuss whether or not you think that, overall, it is worth recycling aluminium.

_____

_____

_____

_____

_____

_____

D One method of recycling plastics involves these steps:

1   Collect mixed plastic waste
2   Separate the plastics by colour
3   Remove paper labels
4   Shred the plastic objects into small pieces

5   Separate the shreds of plastic according to their density
6   Heat the shreds of each type of plastic separately until they melt
7   Cool to make pellets
8   Use the pellets to make new products

Compare the method for recycling plastics to the method for recycling aluminium.

Hint: In your answer, describe how the methods are similar, and then how they are different.

_____

_____

_____

_____

_____

Pinchpoint question

Answer the question below, then do the follow-up activity **with the same letter** as the answer you picked.

Over millions of years, some rock material is recycled from one rock type to another as shown below:

<table>
<tr><td></td><td>1</td><td></td><td>2</td><td></td><td>3</td><td></td></tr>
<tr><td>sedimentary</td><td>⟶</td><td>metamorphic</td><td>⟶</td><td>igneous</td><td>⟶</td><td>sedimentary</td></tr>
</table>

Which order of processes could be correct if the rock material starts in sedimentary rock?

Each arrow above represents one or more processes.

	1	2	3
A	action of pressure makes particles rearrange	melting	weathering, transport, sedimentation, cementation
B	action of heat makes particles rearrange	melting, freezing	weathering, transport, sedimentation, compression
C	action of heat makes rocks melt	melting, freezing	weathering, transport, sedimentation, cementation
D	action of pressure makes particles rearrange	weathering, transport, sedimentation, compression	melting, freezing

Follow-up activities

A Tick the true statements below.

1 Any type of rock (sedimentary, igneous or metamorphic) can melt to form liquid rock. ☐

2 Underground, liquid rock is called lava. ☐

3 On the surface, liquid rock is called magma. ☐

4 Liquid rock cools and melts to form igneous rock. ☐

5 When liquid rock cools quickly the crystals of igneous rock are small. ☐

6 When liquid rock cools slowly the crystals of igneous rock are big. ☐

Hint: The formation of igneous rock from existing rock involves two changes of state. See C2 4.3 Igneous and metamorphic rocks for help.

B Some of the sentences below include one or more mistakes.
Read the sentences and correct the mistakes.

The conversion of metamorphic rock to igneous rock involves evaporating and freezing.

Sedimentary rock may be formed from igneous rock by these processes occurring in this order: weathering, sedimentation, transport, cementation.

The conversion of metamorphic rock to sedimentary rock involves the rearrangement of particles as a result of the action of heat or high pressure.

The conversion of igneous rock to sedimentary rock may involve these processes occurring in this order: transport, weathering, sedimentation, compression.

Metamorphic rock may be formed from igneous rock as a result of the action of low pressure.

Sedimentary rock forms igneous rock when it freezes and then melts.

Igneous and sedimentary rock consist of crystals.

Hint: Read the sentences carefully, and – on scrap paper – start by noting down the starting and ending rock type in each sentence. See C2 4.2 Sedimentary rocks and C2 4.3 Igneous and metamorphic rocks for help.

C a The sentences below can be reordered to describe how metamorphic rock is formed.
Read the statements and write down the order of statements you think will give the best description.

Correct order: ☐ ☐ ☐ ☐ ☐ ☐ ☐ ☐

1 Slate.

2 In this way, limestone turns into…

3 Crystals form, making new – metamorphic – rock.

4 In some places, existing rock is subjected to heat and/or pressure.

5 And mudstone turns into…

6 Marble.

7 Even though the rock does not melt, its particles are rearranged.

8 This new metamorphic rock has a different structure, and some different properties, to the sedimentary rock is was made from.

b Draw a line from each description of processes to show the type of rock that is formed as a result of these processes.

Description of processes

| Rock is broken up to make small pieces of rock. The small pieces of rock move away and are deposited. They join together by compaction or cementation. |

| Rock is heated. It does not melt, but its particles are rearranged. |

| Rock is heated. It melts and freezes again. |

| Rock experiences high pressures. Its particles are rearranged. |

Type of rock that is formed

| igneous |

| metamorphic |

| sedimentary |

Hint: See C2 4.3 Igneous and metamorphic rocks for help.

D Draw **two** lines from each rock type to show some of the processes involved in forming rock of that type.

Rock type

| igneous |

| metamorphic |

| sedimentary |

Processes

| freezing |

| transport |

| action of high pressure makes particles rearrange |

| cementation |

| melting |

| action of high temperature makes particles rearrange without melting |

Hint: Which rock type is formed from liquid rock? See C2 4.2 Sedimentary rocks and C2 4.3 Igneous and metamorphic rocks for help.

Pinchpoint review

Now look back at the question – do you think you chose the right letter?
Turn to the Answers page to find out.

C2 Revision questions

1 🧪🧪 On Earth, carbon is stored in carbon reservoirs. Name **four** of these reservoirs. (*4 marks*)

_____

_____

2 🧪🧪 A student has 95 g of water. He adds sugar to the water and makes a solution. The mass of the solution is 102 g.

a Name the solute in the solution. (*1 mark*)

_____

b Calculate the mass of sugar added to the water. (*2 marks*)

_____ g

3 🧪🧪 Many types of sedimentary rock are porous.

a Explain what porous means. (*1 mark*)

_____

b Explain why a sedimentary rock is porous. (*1 mark*)

_____

_____

4 🧪🧪 Here is part of the reactivity series, in decreasing order of reactivity.

magnesium
zinc
iron
lead
copper
silver

Which **two** pairs of substances take part in displacement reactions? Tick **two** boxes. (*2 marks*)

copper and silver nitrate solution ☐
iron and zinc nitrate solution ☐
lead and iron chloride solution ☐
magnesium and copper chloride solution ☐

5 🧪🧪 A teacher has samples of three metals: potassium, calcium, and magnesium.

a Describe an experiment the teacher could do to compare the reactivity of the three metals.

In your answer, identify **two** control variables and explain how the observations will show which metal is most reactive. (*4 marks*)

_____

_____

_____

_____

_____

_____

b Suggest **one** safety precaution the teacher should take in the experiment you described in part **a**, other than wearing eye protection. (*1 mark*)

_____

6 🧪🧪 In the rock cycle, the materials that make up rocks are recycled. Describe how the conversions below may occur.

a Sedimentary rock to igneous rock. (Involves two stages) (*2 marks*)

_____

_____

b Igneous rock to sedimentary rock. (Involves four stages) (*4 marks*)

_____

_____

_____

_____

7 🧪🧪 Lithium reacts with oxygen gas to make lithium oxide, which is in the solid state at room temperature. Write a balanced symbol equation for the reaction. Use the formulae below and include state symbols.

Formulae: Li O_2 Li_2O (*2 marks*)

Hint: When balancing chemical equations, do not change the formulae.

_____

8 🧪🧪 Compare the **composition** and **properties** of the Earth's inner core and outer core. (*3 marks*)

_____

_____

_____

_____

Hint: In your answer, write down how the inner and outer core are similar, and how they are different.

9 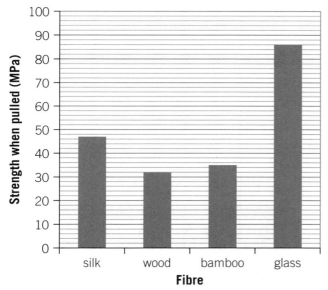 The bar charts in **Figure 1** shows the strength of four composite materials. Each composite is made from poly(ethene) reinforced by a different fibre.

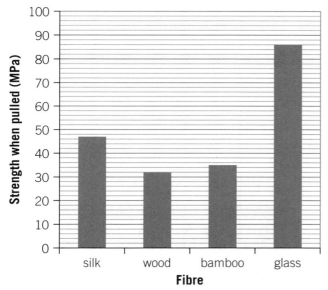

Figure 1

Compare the strengths of wood-reinforced poly(ethene) and glass-reinforced poly(ethene).

Include a calculation in your answer. *(2 marks)*

_____

_____

10 Compare the ways in which igneous and metamorphic rocks are formed. *(3 marks)*

_____

_____

_____

_____

11 Describe and explain **two** impacts of global warming. *(4 marks)*

_____

_____

_____

_____

_____

_____

12 Zinc is extracted from its ore.

a 500 kg of zinc ore is extracted from a mine in China. The ore contains 45 kg of zinc.

Calculate the percentage of zinc in the ore.

(2 marks)

_____ %

b In Europe, zinc used to be extracted from its oxide by heating with carbon monoxide. The equation for the reaction is:

$$ZnO + CO \rightarrow Zn + CO_2$$

i Name the product that is formed in the gas state. *(1 mark)*

_____

ii Suggest why this process is not now used in Europe. *(1 mark)*

_____

_____

13 Draw a line to match each particle diagram to its description. *(3 marks)*

Particle diagram	Description
	a mixture of two compounds
	a pure element
	a mixture of two elements
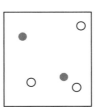	a mixture of an element and a compound

14 🧪🧪🧪 **Table 1** and **Table 2** give data for one physical property of the elements in Group 1 and Group 0 of the Periodic Table. The elements are listed in the same order in the Periodic Table.

Table 1

Group 1 element	Melting point (°C)
lithium	180
sodium	98
potassium	64
rubidium	39

Table 2

Group 0 element	Melting point (°C)
helium	−270
neon	−249
argon	−189
krypton	−157

Use data from **Table 1** and **Table 2**, and your own knowledge, to compare the patterns in two physical properties and one chemical property of the elements in Group 1 and Group 0. *(6 marks)*

_____

_____

_____

_____

_____

_____

_____

_____

15 🧪🧪🧪 The word equations show how two Group 1 elements react with chlorine.

lithium + chlorine → lithium chloride

potassium + chlorine → potassium chloride

a Rubidium is also in Group 1, just below potassium. Predict the name of the product of the reaction between rubidium and chlorine. *(1 mark)*

_____

b Predict which element reacts most vigorously with chlorine: lithium, potassium, or rubidium. *(1 mark)*

_____

c Explain the prediction you made in part **b**. *(1 mark)*

_____

d The balanced symbol equation for the reaction of lithium and chlorine is $2Li + Cl_2 \rightarrow 2LiCl$

Write the balanced symbol equation for the reaction of rubidium with chlorine. Use these formulae: Rb, Cl_2, $RbCl$ *(2 marks)*

_____

16 **Table 3** shows the properties of three materials, **X**, **Y**, and **Z**. *(1 mark)*

Table 3

Material	Melting point (°C)	Does it conduct electricity?	Is it brittle?
X	3130	yes	no
Y	4215	no	yes
Z	from 120 to 180	no	no

a Write down the letter of one material in the table that could be a ceramic. *(1 mark)*

_____

b Justify your choice in part **a**. *(1 mark)*

_____

_____

Hint: 'Justify' means that you have to use evidence from **Table 3** to support your answer.

c Write down the letter of one material in the table that could be a polymer. *(1 mark)*

_____

d Suggest **one** other property that the material your chose in part **c** may have, other than the properties listed in the table. *(1 mark)*

_____

C2 Checklist

Revision question number	Outcome	Topic reference	😞	😐	😊
1	Use the carbon cycle to identify reservoirs of carbon.	C2 4.5			
2a	Describe solutions using key words.	C2 2.2			
2b	Use data to predict how much solute is dissolved in a solution or the mass of a solution.	C2 2.2			
3	Explain two properties of sedimentary rock.	C2 4.2			
4	Predict if a given pair of substances will undergo displacement.	C2 3.4			
5	Compare the reactions of metals with water.	C2 3.3 WS 1.1			
6	Use the rock cycle to explain how the material in rocks is recycled.	C2 4.4			
7	Use state symbols in balanced formula equations.	C2 3.2			
8	Compare the different layers of the Earth in terms of their properties.	C2 4.1			
9	Use data to compare the properties of composite materials.	C2 3.8			
10	Compare the ways that igneous and metamorphic rocks form.	C2 4.3			
11	Explain some impacts of global warming.	C2 4.6			
12	Convert amounts of metals within ores from masses to percentages.	C2 3.5			
13	Interpret particle models that represent mixtures and pure substances.	C2 2.1			
14	Compare the patterns in properties of Group 0 elements with those in Group 1.	C2 1.3 C2 1.5			
15	Use experimental observations to explain reactivity trends in Group 1.	C2 1.3			
16a, b	Justify the choice of ceramic materials from data about material properties.	C2 3.6			
16c, d	Describe polymer properties.	C2 3.7			

P1.1 Charging up

A Atoms contain equal numbers of _____ (+) and _____(–), so overall, atoms have a _____ charge. When two objects are rubbed together, _____ move _____ from one object to the other, making one object _____ charged and the other object positively charged. Charged objects are surrounded by an _____ _____. If two charged objects have the same type of charge, they _____ each other. If two charged objects have the opposite type of charge (one + and one –), they _____ each other. Thunderstorms generate very strong electric fields, which cause _____ .

B **a** Complete the sentences below to explain how objects can become charged.

Atoms are made of positive and negative particles. _____ separates charge. When the objects are rubbed together, this moves _____ from one material to the other. The material that lost _____ now has _____ charge overall. The other material has _____ charge.

b A series of objects have been charged with friction.
Complete the table to show which pairs of objects will attract, repel, or have no effect on each other.

Pair	1st object charge	2nd object charge	Attract, repel, or no effect?
A	positive	positive	
B	positive	negative	
C	negative	positive	
D	negative	negative	

C Static electricity can be used to improve spray painting of a car in a factory, as shown in this diagram.

a Circle what happens as the neutral paint droplets pass the positive tip of the spray gun.

paint droplets gain electrons   nothing

paint droplets lose electrons

nozzle of spray gun is positively charged

paint particles become positively charged

the car has a negative charge

b **i** Circle a prediction for how the charged paint particles will interact with the car.

paint droplets attracted to car   paint droplets neither attracted nor repelled

paint droplets repelled by car

ii Suggest why this technique is better than spray painting without using electricity.

_____

D An electron is surrounded by an electric field, like the Earth is surrounded by a gravitational field. Give one similarity and one difference between these two types of field.

Similarity: _____

_____

Difference: _____

_____

P1.2 Circuits and current

A Negatively charged _____ move when current flows in a metal. Current is the amount of charge

flowing per _____. We use an _____ to measure current in an electrical circuit.

It must be connected in _____ so that all of the current that flows through the component

of interest also flows through the _____. The unit of current is the ampere, often abbreviated

to _____, with the symbol _____. A component that can push charge around

a circuit is a _____ or _____. A component that can make an object move is a

_____ . A device that can break and complete a circuit is a _____. A circuit must be

_____ for the charge to flow around it.

B A scientist decides to investigate the amount of electrical current needed to power different types of light bulb. She sets up a circuit for each lightbulb as shown.

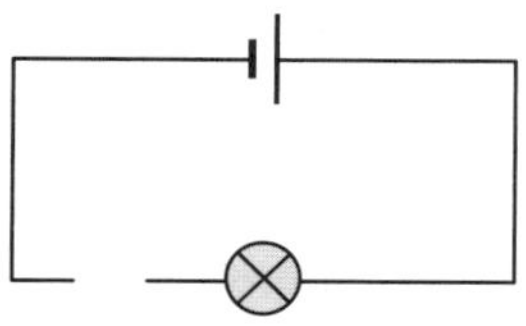

a Complete the circuit to show how she can measure the current that the bulb needs.

b Tick the correct way in which the component in part **a** needs to be added to the circuit:

series ☐

parallel ☐

c Define the term 'current'.

_____

C The diagram shows a simple circuit.

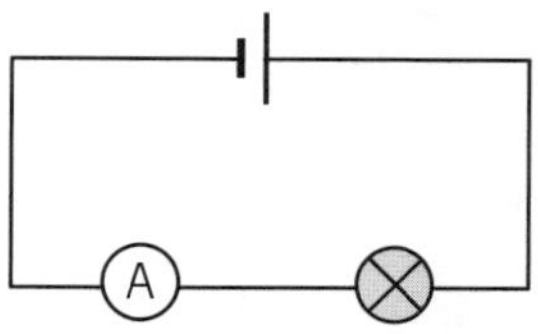

The cell in this circuit is kept the same while more bulbs are added in series.

What will happen to the current in this circuit?

_____

D a One model of electricity uses a loop of rope as shown.

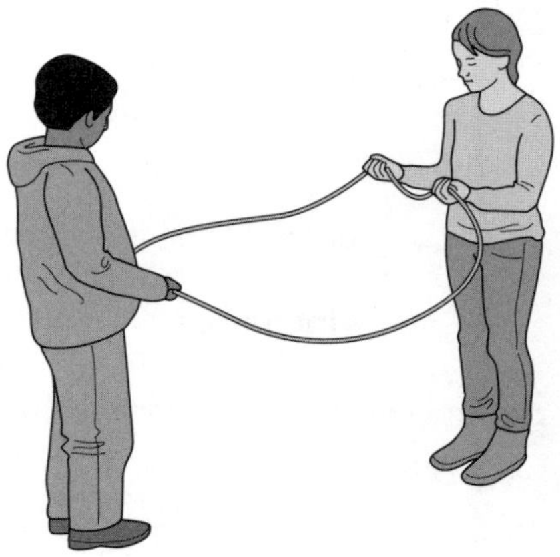

One person acts as a cell, pulling the rope around, through the hands of the person acting as a bulb.

i What electrical concept does a piece of the rope represent?

_____

ii What represents current in the model?

_____

b The person acting as a bulb represents greater resistance by gripping the rope harder so that the rope moves more slowly. Describe what has changed in terms of the charges in the circuit.

_____

P1.3 Potential difference

A Cells or batteries provide a push to charges in a circuit to make them move. This is called the _____

_____ . We use a _____ to measure potential difference. It must be connected

in _____ so that it is across the component we are interested in. Potential difference is

measured in _____, with symbol_____, so potential difference is often known as

_____. Cells and batteries are given a _____, which is the potential difference across

the cell / battery. A _____ potential difference means that more _____is transferred to

the components in a circuit than if the potential difference is _____.

B **a** Draw a circuit diagram to show how you would measure potential difference across a bulb.

b Fill in the gaps to complete the sentences about potential difference.

Potential difference (p.d.) means the 'push' provided by the _____ (that is, the energy that it can

provide). Another term commonly used for p.d. is _____. The amount of potential difference that

a _____ provides is measured in _____.

C Draw a line to match each variable with its properties and behaviour in a series circuit.

Current		Total for all components same as rating for cell		Relates to charge flowing

Potential difference		Same everywhere		Relates to energy transferred to a component

D The diagram shows a simple circuit.

The bulb is kept the same in this circuit while the cell is replaced by one with a higher rating.

Circle your prediction for what will happen to the current.

increases	**stays the same**	**decreases**

E Explain why an ammeter must be connected in series, but a voltmeter must be connected in parallel.

_____

_____

_____

_____

P1.4 Series and parallel

A There are two types of electrical circuits. _____ circuits have all their components, including the

cell, in one loop, so that there is only one path for the current to follow. As you add more components, the current

gets _____ . _____ is the same everywhere. If you add up the _____

_____ across each component, the sum is equal to the _____ _____

across the cell.

_____ circuits have their components in more than one loop, so there are at least two different paths

for the current to follow. As you add more loops, each with their own components, the total current through the

cell gets _____ . If you add up the _____ through each loop, the sum is equal to the

_____ through the cell. The _____ _____ across each loop is the same

as that across the cell.

B The diagrams below show some simple series and parallel circuits, including some readings on ammeters and
voltmeters. Write in the missing readings.

a series potential difference

b parallel current

c parallel potential difference

C In British houses, several mains electricity sockets are connected together using a 'ring main'.

Suggest whether these sockets are connected in series and parallel in a ring main. Explain your answer.

_____

_____

D The law of conservation of charge says that it cannot be created or destroyed.

Explain how this law applies to each type of circuit.

Series_____

_____

Parallel_____

_____

P1.5 Resistance

A _____ is a measure of how much 'push' is required to get current through a component. Strictly, it is defined and calculated as the _____ _____ across a component divided by the _____ through that component. It has the unit _____ , symbol Ω. If 1 V applied across a component causes 1 A to flow, we say that the component has a _____ of 1 Ω. Insulators have very _____ resistance and conductors have very _____ resistance.

B Resistance can be calculated using the following formula:

$$\text{resistance } (\Omega) = \frac{\text{potential difference (V)}}{\text{current (A)}}$$

Calculate the resistance of the bulb in the circuit shown to the right. Give the unit.

_____

6.0 V

0.20 A

C a Rearrange the formula for resistance to give the formula for calculating current.

_____

b Calculate the current flowing through this cell.

$R = 30\ \Omega$ 9.0 V

_____

D a Rearrange the formula for resistance to calculate potential difference.

_____

b Calculate the potential difference across this bulb.

$R = 20\ \Omega$

0.50 A

_____

E One problem with the copper metal used to make electrical wires is that it has some resistance.

Explain the cause of this resistance.

_____

_____

F Draw a line to link each factor with its effect on the resistance of a wire and the explanation.

Increasing length of wire	decreases resistance	because there are more paths along which the electrons can travel through the vibrating particles
Increasing diameter of wire	increases resistance	because each electron collides with more vibrating particles as it passes along the wire

G Explain how and why the resistance of the wiring in a hairdryer differs from the resistance of its outer plastic coating.

_____

_____

P1.6 Magnets and magnetic fields

A Some materials are attracted to a magnet , or can be themselves turned into permanent _____ . These are called _____ _____ , and include the elements _____ , nickel, and cobalt, and some types of steel, which contains _____ . Every magnet has a _____ _____ and a _____ _____ . A compass is a magnet that is free to rotate. It will spin until its _____ seeking pole points to the _____ north pole, which is actually a magnetic _____ pole. Two magnets will attract each other if they have _____ poles nearest to each other, or repel if they have the _____ poles nearest to each other. We say that magnets are surrounded by a _____ _____ , which we can detect using a compass or iron filings. We can represent this by drawing _____ _____ _____ , which point from the north-seeking pole to the south-seeking pole, and show where a field is strong by drawing _____ of them.

B For each combination of magnets below, write whether they will attract, repel, or have no effect.

a | **N** | | **S** | _____

b | **S** | | **N** | _____

c | **N** | | **N** | _____

d | **S** | | **S** | _____

C It is possible to use a pair of magnets as a fastener on a bag. People with limited mobility in their hands can find these fasteners particularly easy to use.

Explain how two magnets can be used to hold a bag closed.

_____

_____

D a Complete this diagram to show the magnetic field lines around a bar magnet.

b On your diagram for part **a**, add two labels to the magnetic field:

- **W** to show a weaker part of the field.

- **S** to show a stronger part of the field.

| N | | S |

c Describe what it means when magnetic field lines are shown closer together.

_____

E Lara is a physicist who needs to find which direction is north.

Describe how she can use a magnet to do so.

_____

_____

_____

P1.7 Electromagnets

A An electromagnet consists of a _____ of wire with many _____, wrapped around a _____. To make an electromagnet stronger, create _____ _____ on the coil, use a larger _____, or use a _____ in the core that is easy to _____, such as iron. Electromagnets can be more useful than _____ magnets because they can be _____ _____ or made far stronger. The magnetic _____ around an electromagnet is very similar to that around a _____ magnet.

B Fill in the gaps using these keywords to explain how an electromagnet works. You may use the keywords once, more than once, or not at all.

core   **field**   **doesn't**   **current**

magnetic material   **magnetic field**   **coil**   **does**

An electromagnet consists of a _____ passing through a _____ of wire, usually wrapped around an iron _____. This creates a _____ _____. If the _____ is switched off then the electromagnet _____ pick up magnetic material.

C Describe **two** ways to make an electromagnet stronger.

_____

_____

D A physicist carries out a set of experiments on the strength of an electromagnet by making the following changes.

- Increase current

- Remove magnetic core

- Decrease number of turns on coil

- Reverse direction of current

For each variable she changes, predict and explain whether the strength of the electromagnet will become weaker, become stronger, or stay the same.

_____

_____

_____

_____

_____

_____

_____

_____

P1.8 Using electromagnets

A One device that uses electromagnetism to make things move is a _____ . A simple one consists of a _____ of wire near a pair of _____ _____ . Once connected to a power supply, a _____ flows. The coil acts as an _____ , so there are forces between the coil and the permanent magnets, making the coil _____ . Another device is a _____ . This uses a small current in one circuit to control a _____ current in another _____ . When the user closes a switch, a coil becomes an _____ . Two pieces of iron inside the coil are _____ . They attract each other, touching and _____ the other circuit. This is useful for _____ , so that the person controlling the current can be kept further away from large currents or potential differences.

B The statements below can be reordered to correctly describe how a simple motor works.

Write the order of the statements that gives the best description.

Correct order ☐ ☐ ☐ ☐

1 Current flows in coil.

2 Connect coil to a battery.

3 Coil becomes an electromagnet.

4 Forces between the coil and the permanent magnet make the coil spin.

C You are provided with a long piece of wire, a 10-cm-long iron bar, a cell, and a switch.
Describe how you would use these items to separate magnetic materials in a model recycling plant.
Include a circuit diagram in your answer and explain why a switch is essential.

_____

_____

_____

_____

D A physicist carries out a series of experiments to test the effect of changing certain variables on the speed of a motor. Using your knowledge of electromagnets, suggest whether each of the following changes will make the motor turn faster or slower.

a Decreasing the current _____

b Inserting a magnetic core into the coil _____

c Increasing the number of turns in the coil _____

E An X-ray machine in a hospital is powered using a battery of many cells. For safety, it is controlled using a relay with a single cell.

Draw a circuit diagram for this equipment. (You may represent the X-ray machine with a box with those words in.)

Pinchpoint question

Answer the question below, then do the follow-up activity **with the same letter** as the answer you picked.

The circuits in the diagrams below include identical bulbs and cells.

Choose the statement that correctly describes and explains the behaviour of electricity in the circuits.

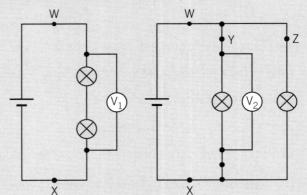

A In both circuits, the current at **X** must be less than the current at **W** because it is used up going through the bulbs.

B Each bulb in the series circuit is brighter than each bulb in the parallel circuit, because all of the current from the cell goes through them.

C The voltmeter reading V_1 must be greater than the voltmeter reading V_2 because each charge has to do more work (transfer more energy) to get through more bulbs.

D In the parallel circuit on the right, the current at **Y** and at **Z** must add up to the current reading at **W**, because electrical charge cannot be created or destroyed.

Follow-up activities

A In a series circuit, the current must be the same everywhere.

Complete the statements below to explain why.

Like energy, charge cannot be _____ or _____, so charge cannot be used up.

If some charge goes into a bulb, then the _____ amount of charge must come out.

Current is the amount of charge _____ per _____.

If some current goes into a bulb, then the _____ amount of current must come out.

As charge cannot be 'used up', neither can _____.

Hint: What is current? See P2 1.2 Circuits and current for help.

B For each question about circuits below, circle your answer.

a In a series circuit, what is the effect on **resistance** of adding more bulbs?

increase / no change / decrease

b In a series circuit, the potential difference across the battery is kept the same. What is the effect on **current** of adding more bulbs?

increase / no change / decrease

c In the diagram below, how does the resistance of the one-bulb branch compare to the two-bulb branch?

higher / same / lower

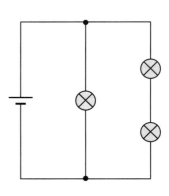

d   In the circuit below, how does the voltage reading of V_1 compare to V_2?

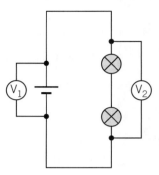

higher / same / lower

Hint: How does current depend on resistance? See P2 1.5 Resistance for help.

C a   Define potential difference.

_____

b   Each statement below contains a mistake. Rewrite each statement to correct it.

i   Potential difference tells you nothing about energy.

_____

ii   The potential difference across all branches of a parallel circuit must be different.

_____

iii   Any one electron must do less work on the components than the work the battery did on it.

_____

iv   The p.d. across all branches in a circuit sometimes adds up to the p.d. across the cell.

_____

Hint: What is potential difference? See P2 1.3 Potential difference for help.

D   In this circuit, the bulbs are all identical, the cell is rated at 3.0 V, and there is 1.2 A of current through the cell.

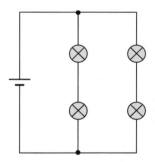

a   What is the potential difference across each of the bulbs? Explain your answer.

_____

_____

b   What is the current through each of the bulbs? Explain your answer.

_____

_____

Hint: How do current and potential difference behave in serial and parallel circuits? See P1.4 Series and parallel for help.

 Pinchpoint review

Now look back at the question – do you think you chose the right letter?
Turn to the Answers page to find out.

A Different foods are stores of different amounts of _____. The unit for this is the _____, and 1000 of them make up one _____. A healthy diet will take in just as much energy as is needed for the person's _____. The body will convert extra food into _____ to store unused energy.

B **a** Draw a line to match each activity with its energy requirement.

b Explain the different energy requirements for sleeping and running.

_____

_____

Sleeping	300 kJ per hour
Running	600 kJ per hour
Working	3600 kJ per hour

C **a** Katie requires 300 kJ of energy to run 1 kilometre.

Calculate the energy she requires for a 20 km training run. _____

b Suggest a meal that meets Katie's energy requirements, using the data in the table.

Food	Energy (kJ) per 100 g
apple	200
banana	340
chicken breast	600
whole wheat pasta	700
chocolate	1500
dried fruit and nut mix	1900

_____

_____

c Katie is preparing to run a 160 km 'ultramarathon'. She will need to consume half of the required energy while running and so wants the food to take up a small volume.

i Calculate how much energy she needs to consume while running.

_____ kJ

ii Suggest the mass of a low-volume food she could eat while running.

_____ g of _____

D A dietician wants to calculate how much energy is needed by a child in one day.

Aiden walks for one hour (800 kJ/h), works for six hours (600 kJ/h), relaxes for five hours (360 kJ/h) and sleeps for twelve hours (300 kJ/h).

Complete the table and calculate the total energy needed for one day.

Activity	Duration (hours)	Energy required for an hour of activity (kJ/h)	Total energy used (kJ)
walking	1		
working	6		
relaxing	5		
sleeping	12		

Total energy used in 24 hours: _____

P2.2 Energy adds up

A Energy cannot be created or destroyed – this is the law of _____ of _____.

Energy transfers between _____ _____, with some stores emptying as others

_____, so that the _____ amount of energy remains the same. Chemicals, such as

fuels or food and the oxygen needed to combust or respire, have a _____ store associated with

them. Hot objects are associated with a _____ store; moving ones with a _____

store; objects above the surface of the Earth with a _____ _____ store; stretched or

compressed ones an _____ store.

In many processes, energy is not only transferred to the store you want it in, but also 'lost' to a store which is not

useful. We say that that energy has _____.

B For each situation below, name the energy stores involved.

   a   Coal is burnt to heat some water.

      _____

   b   Georgia starts her petrol car. It begins to move and then speeds up.

      _____

   c   Charlie freewheels down a hill on his scooter.

      _____

C **a**   A ski lift is powered by a petrol-driven engine, and lifts a skier from the foot of a mountain to its top.

     i   Suggest which energy stores are involved and whether each fills or empties.

       _____

       _____

     ii   Name which of these stores accounts for energy dissipation.

       _____

   b   A power station burns coal. The electricity it produces is used to power a lift, moving two people from the ground floor to the fifth floor of a building.

     i   Describe a form of energy transfer involved in this process.

       _____

     ii   Explain how the changes in the energy stores obey conservation of energy.

       _____

       _____

D David is conducting an experiment to measure the effect of energy dissipation when heating a saucepan of water using different heating methods. David times how long it takes for the temperature of the water to increase by 20 °C. For each source of error, circle whether it is systematic or random, and suggest how to minimise it.

Source of error	Systematic or random?	How to minimise error
Left lid off saucepan	**systematic / random**	
Thermometer reading	**systematic / random**	
Timing	**systematic / random**	

P2.3 Energy and temperature

A We describe how hot or cold something is as its _____. We measure this using a

_____, using the unit of _____ _____, symbol _____.

If a hotter object is put in contact with a colder one, the hot one will heat the cold one until they reach

the _____ temperature and are in _____ , that is until _____

_____ energy is transferred between their _____ stores.

The energy that you need to raise the temperature of a material depends on the _____ of material

and the _____ of material, as well as on how much you want to raise the temperature.

B **a** When an object is heated, both its temperature and the energy in its thermal store increase.
Use the words in the list below to complete the following sentences about temperature and energy.

| **increases** | **J** | **°C** | **move / vibrate** | **thermal** | **increases** | **stays the same** |

Temperature is measured in _____. As the mass of an object changes, its temperature

_____. As temperature _____, the particles that make up the object

_____ more.

Energy is measured in _____. As the mass of the object increases, the amount of energy in its

_____ store _____.

b Circle the **bold** words to complete the following sentences about heat and thermal energy .

A cup of tea at 80 °C has **more / less** thermal energy than a very large swimming pool that is at 30 °C.

The cup of tea is **hotter / colder** than the swimming pool, but the large swimming pool has **more / less**

thermal energy.

C Suggest and explain which you expect to have a larger thermal store of energy: one cubic metre of water or one
cubic metre of air at the same temperature.

_____

_____

D For each of the following situations, explain whether equilibrium has been reached.

a A person outside shivering in the cold.

_____

b A cup of tea that has been left in a room overnight.

_____

c A thermometer in a patient's mouth for a minute.

_____

P2.4 Energy transfer: particles

A Energy can be transferred by heating – this transfers the energy from a _____ store associated with a _____ object into the thermal store of a _____ object. This can happen in three ways.

Particles in a hot material _____. When they collide with their neighbours, making them vibrate, we call that _____. This process happens fastest with materials in a _____ state and slowest with materials in a _____ state.

When you heat a liquid or gas, its particles move further apart so the fluid becomes less _____. The hotter, less _____ fluid then rises, moving to a place which is colder. This process is called _____. The movement of the fluid is called a _____ _____.

B **a** The photograph shows an example of conduction.
Explain how energy is transferred during conduction.

_____

_____

b The image shows a pan of soup being heated on a stove, which is an example of convection.

Reorder these statements to explain the process of convection.

Correct order: ☐ ☐ ☐ ☐

1 The heated particles move further apart, so the liquid becomes less dense.
2 The lower density liquid moves upwards through colder liquid.
3 The more dense colder liquid sinks and these particles are then heated at the base of the pan.
4 Heating a liquid particle makes it move and vibrate faster.

C Fill in the gaps using the keywords below to explain why certain materials are good insulators.

solids	gases	thermal	weak	gas	far apart	non-metals

_____ are good _____ insulators because their particles are _____

_____, with _____ forces between them. Some _____ are also good

insulators such as many _____, like wood and certain plastics. Many of the best insulators are

_____ which trap little pockets of _____.

D Lexi carries out an experiment to see which cup is best at keeping drinks cold. She measures the time it takes for a cold drink to warm by 10 °C. To make it a fair test, all the cups contained the same volume of liquid at the same starting temperature, had the same colour and finish on the outside, and the same lid. The table shows her results.

Cup	Time to warm by 10 °C (hours)
Tough, solid, steel	0.5
Expanded polystyrene foam	3.0
Two layers of plastic separated by a vacuum	6.0

Use your knowledge of insulators and conductors to compare and explain these results.

_____

_____

_____

P2.5 Energy transfer: radiation

A To transfer energy by _____ or _____ requires particles. However, these are not needed for heating by _____. Hot objects emit _____ _____, sometimes known as thermal radiation or heat. This can be detected using a _____ _____ _____, for instance to help firefighters find people in a smoke-filled room. When objects _____ this radiation, they warm up. It is a wave like light and can be _____, _____, or _____. Surfaces which have a _____ colour and _____ finish absorb infrared better than ones which are _____ and _____. The best absorbers are also the best emitters, so _____, _____ surfaces emit the most infrared.

B **a** Draw a line to match each method of energy transfer with its cause.

Conduction		Emission and absorption of infrared
Convection		Particles moving from a hotter place to a colder place
Radiation		In solids, particles vibrating and colliding with neighbours

b Explain how energy is transferred by radiation using these keywords:

radiation	**emit**	**absorb**	**infrared**	**hot objects**	**heating**

_____

_____

_____

_____

c Suggest one piece of evidence that radiation does not need particles to transfer energy.

_____

Hint: What do you feel when you turn your face to the Sun?

C The diagram shows a 'heat sink', used to cool computer components.

Explain why it is good for this task.

_____

_____

D Willow is planning to carry out an experiment involving boiling water in a beaker and measuring its temperature whilst cooling. Her risk assessment at the moment reads 'Risk of burning yourself on hot equipment'.

Suggest a control measure to reduce this risk.

_____

_____

P2.6 Energy resources

A Anything that can be used as a fuel or to generate electricity is an _____ _____.

Coal, oil, and gas are examples of _____ _____. These cannot be readily replaced,

so they are _____. Fuels can be burnt to heat water and turn a turbine to generate electricity in

a _____ _____ _____. Some energy resources such as wind and

solar are continually being produced and are _____. When fossil fuels are burnt, they produce

_____ _____ which contributes to climate change and _____

_____ which contributes to acid rain. When renewable sources such as wind and solar are in use,

they do not produce these polluting gases.

B **a** Name an energy resource that can be used in a thermal power station, other than coal.

_____

b Write the order of these statements which gives the best description of how coal is used in a thermal power station to generate electricity for your home.

Correct order ☐ ☐ ☐ ☐ ☐ ☐

   1 steam, which drives a…

   2 Coal is burnt, which heats…

   3 electrical current to power your home

   4 turbine, which turns a…

   5 water, to produce…

   6 generator, which pushes…

C List the advantages of using renewable and non-renewable resources, giving at least one advantage for each.

_____

_____

_____

_____

D A student carried out an experiment to see how a solar panel cell's output varied with its distance from a bright bulb. He set up his experiment as shown in the diagram.

He measured the distance from the nearest part of the bulb, rather than from the centre of the bulb.

Explain how this is likely to affect his results and whether this causes a random or systematic error.

_____

_____

_____

_____

clamp

bulb

retort stand

ruler

solar cell

A Power (in W) is defined and calculated as the _____ transferred (J) divided by the

_____ taken for that transfer (s). If one joule of _____ is transferred in one second,

then the _____ produced is one watt (W). In electrical circuits, power can be calculated as the

_____ times the _____ _____. Electrical devices are often labelled with

a _____ _____. This shows the amount of power they can produce. The unit for this is

the _____ with the symbol W, and 1000 of them make up one _____, symbol kW.

If you use a device that produces one kilowatt of power for one hour, you will have transferred one

_____ _____ of energy, symbol kW h.

B Recall the correct equation for each of the questions below.

   a   A gas stove runs for 30 s and burns fuel of energy 45 000 J.
       Calculate the power produced by the gas stove.

_____

   b **i**   A hairdryer requires a current of 10 A and operates at 230 V.
          Calculate the power produced by the hairdryer.

_____

      ii   Calculate how much energy is transferred by the hairdryer in 30 s.

_____

   c   An electrical radiator to heat a room is rated at 2 kW.
       Calculate the energy transferred when the radiator heats a room for four hours.

_____

C Harper lights her front room with a 75 W light bulb. It is on for 4 hours per day and Harper pays 15 p per kW h
for electricity.

   a   Calculate the cost in pence of using the bulb for one year. There are 365 days in a year.

_____

   b   An LED bulb of equivalent brightness has a power of 11 W.

       Calculate the cost in pence of using an LED bulb for one year.

_____

   c   Calculate the reduction in Harper's energy bill, in pounds, if she uses an LED bulb instead.

_____

P2.8 Work, energy, and machines

A When an object is moved by a force through a distance, we say that _____ is done. It is a way

of transferring _____, like heating. Work _____ is defined and calculated as the

force (N) times the distance moved (m). It has the same unit as energy, the _____, symbol J. If a

_____ of one newton moves an object one metre, then one joule of _____ was done,

and one joule of _____ was transferred between stores. Devices that reduce the force needed to

move an object, or increase the distance the object moves when you apply a force, are called _____

_____. Examples include _____, pulleys, and _____.

B a A mechanic applies a force of 120 N to a lever to lift a car, moving the lever through a distance of 0.40 m.
Calculate the work he does on the lever.

_____

   b The mechanic has done work on the lever. To lift the car, the lever must do work on the car.
Suggest the maximum work that the lever can do on the car and give a reason.

_____

C A machine that lifts a load to place it on a shelf in a warehouse is operated by a
foot pump.

A load of 1500 N needs to be raised by 1.0 m.

   a Calculate the work done if Ethan lifts that load himself.

_____

   b Lifting the load 1.0 m requires 30 presses of the foot pump, each needing Ethan to do 50 J of work (ignoring the
effect of friction).

Calculate the work done by Ethan using the machine.

_____

   c Explain how the principle of conservation of energy applies to Ethan lifting the load by 1.0 m using the lift table,
using each of these keywords at least once.

chemical store	gravitational store	thermal store	equal	fills	empties

_____

_____

_____

_____

Pinchpoint question

Answer the question below, then do the follow-up activity **with the same letter** as the answer you picked.

Parker lives in a remote area and it is winter. He uses an electrical generator that burns diesel fuel to power the electrical devices in his home, including his heaters. The thermostat keeps his home at a constant temperature.

Which statement about the energy transfers involved in one hour of running the generator is correct? The house remains at the temperature set by the thermostat during this time.

A The chemical store of the fuel is used up to fill the thermal energy store of the house. As the house cools, the thermal energy store of the house is used up. The thermal store outside the home does not change.

B The chemical store of the fuel empties as the current from the generator does work on the heaters. The thermal store of the surroundings fills due to heating from the warm home, filling by as much as the chemical store empties.

C Parker has plugged in his mobile phone to charge it. This fills the electrical energy store of the phone battery.

D The chemical store of the fuel empties. The heaters fill the thermal store of the house. The increase in the thermal store of the house is equal to the loss from the chemical store.

Follow-up activities

A Complete the sentences using the keywords below. You may use each word more than once.

constant	fill	warmer	rate	empties	heated	fills

a The diagram shows a hot saucepan that has been put in cooler water.

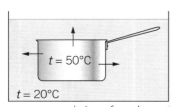

energy is transferred

The saucepan is _____ than the water. The water will be _____ by the

saucepan. The thermal store of the saucepan _____ and the thermal store of the water

_____. Whenever a thermal store empties, another store must _____.

b A house with a thermostat stays at a constant temperature. This means the thermal store of the house stays

at a _____ level. Once the house has reached the temperature set by the thermostat, as the

chemical store of the fuel _____, energy is transferred into and out of the house's thermal store

at the same _____. The thermal store of the surroundings _____ because the

house is _____ than its surroundings.

Hint: What is a thermal store? See P2 2.2 Energy adds up for help.

B Parker sets the house's thermostat to a higher temperature.
Describe and explain the effect this has on the thermal store of the surroundings.

_____

_____

_____

_____

Hint: Which stores change and why? See P2 2.2 Energy adds up for help.

C Complete the sentences about the house using the words below. You may use each word more than once.

store	dissipation	fuel	thermal
work	surroundings	water	chemical

The electrical circuits in the house are just a way for the generator to do _____ on various devices, such as the heater. Electricity is not a _____ of energy in this situation.

When Parker boils a kettle of water, the _____ store of the _____ is emptying and the _____ store of the _____ is filling. When he recharges his phone battery, the _____ store of the _____ is emptying and the _____ store of the battery is filling. In both cases, there is also _____, as the thermal store of the _____ fills.

Hint: Which stores are involved with a generator? See P2 2.6 Energy resources for help.

D Several electrical heaters are used to heat Parker's house. They are controlled by thermostats so that after one hour the house is still at the same temperature.

Circle whether each statement is true or false.

a Heating involves a hotter object (the house) heating a cooler object (the surroundings). **true / false**

b The temperature of the house is different after one hour. **true / false**

c The amount of energy in an object's thermal store relates to its temperature. **true / false**

d If the temperature of an object changes, the amount of energy in its thermal store does not change. **true / false**

e The house is hotter than its surroundings so the thermal store of the surroundings will increase. **true / false**

f After an hour, the thermal store of the house will be filling and emptying at a constant rate. **true / false**

Hint: Which stores are involved in heating? See P2 2.2 Energy adds up for help.

Pinchpoint review

Now look back at the question – do you think you chose the right letter?
Turn to the Answers page to find out.

P3.1 Speed

A The rate at which something moves is called _____. It is defined and calculated as the _____ travelled (m) divided by the time taken (s). It has the unit _____ _____, symbol m/s. If something moves a _____ of one metre in one second, then it has a _____ of one m/s. We can distinguish between the _____ that something has just at one moment – its _____ _____ – and its _____ _____ over a whole journey. When two objects are moving, we can talk about their _____ _____. For instance, two people walking at the same speed of 1.5 m/s would have a _____ _____ of zero if they are walking in the same direction, but a _____ _____ of 3 m/s if they are walking in opposite directions.

B Average speed can be calculated if you know the distance travelled and the time taken. Recall the formula for speed to answer these questions.

   a A motorbike drives a distance of 500 m in a time of 30 s.

      Calculate its average speed.

      _____

   b The formula for speed can be used with different units.

      A train travels 160 km in 2.0 h. Calculate the average speed.

      _____

   c Rearrange the formula for speed to calculate the distance travelled. The sound of thunder travels at 330 m/s. Calculate how far it will travel in 12 s.

      _____

C One type of traffic speed camera works by taking a pair of photographs 0.50 s apart while the traffic drives over equally spaced, parallel white lines on the road.

The speed limit on the motorway is 31 metres per second (m/s). One pair of photographs shows that a car travelled 20 m in the time between the photographs.

   a Calculate the speed of the car.

      _____

   b Was the car exceeding the speed limit?

      _____

D An airliner is cruising at 900 km/h compared to the air around it. The air itself is moving at 110 km/h as a tailwind, coming from behind the aircraft.

   a Explain what is meant by the relative speed of the airliner and the ground.

      _____

      _____

direction of wind

   b Calculate the relative speed of the airliner to the ground.

      _____

P3.2 Motion graphs

A One way to describe a journey is to plot a _____–_____ graph. If an object is not

moving, the graph stays _____. The slope of the graph shows its _____. If the object's

speed is changing, we say it is _____.

B a Lola carries out an experiment on a wind-up moving toy, measuring the distance it travels three times. Her results are shown in the table below.

Time (s)	Distance 1st reading (m)	Distance 2nd reading (m)	Distance 3rd reading (m)	Average distance (m)
0	0.00	0.00	0.00	
5	0.04	0.02	0.05	
10	0.11	0.12	0.12	
15	0.26	0.31	0.26	
20	0.43	0.48	0.40	
25	0.60	0.63	0.58	
30	0.75	0.80	0.74	
35	0.78	0.83	0.80	
40	0.78	0.83	0.81	

i Complete the table by calculating the average distance for each time.

ii Plot the data on the axes given and draw a smooth line of best fit.

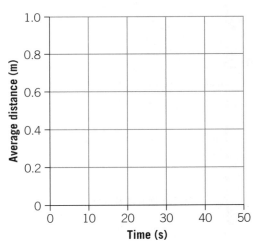

b Describe what is happening to the car between:

i 0 s and 10 s

_____

_____

ii 10 s and 30 s

_____

_____

iii 30 s and 40 s.

_____

_____

c Calculate the maximum speed of the toy from the graph.

_____

P3.3 Pressure in gases

A Gases, such as air, exert _____ _____ because of collisions between the gas

_____, and between them and any surface they touch. When we squeeze a gas it is

_____, which increases its pressure and its _____. The air around us is at

_____ _____, which causes a force pushing in on our skin. This is balanced by the

pressure from inside our bodies. As you go higher, such as up a mountain, _____

_____ gets _____.

B Draw a line to match each factor with its effect on pressure and the reason.

| An increase in **temperature** | causes an **increase** in pressure | because the particles have **further** to travel so collide **less** often. |

| An increase in **volume** | causes a **decrease** in pressure | because the gas particles move **faster**, so collide **harder** and **more** often. |

C Aerosol cans sold in the UK normally have this warning: "Protect from sunlight and do not expose to temperatures exceeding 50 °C."

Use the concepts of gas pressure inside the can and atmospheric pressure outside the can to explain why this warning is needed.

_____

_____

_____

_____

D La Paz is the highest-altitude capital city in the world, at 3640 m. At that altitude, atmospheric pressure is significantly lower, and therefore air is less dense.

Draw a line to match each effect with its cause.

| You can kick a football further because | | there is less oxygen per litre. |

| Athletes cannot run as far or as fast because | | neighbouring air particles collide with each other less often. |

| The speed of sound is lower because | | air particles collide with objects less often so there is less drag. |

E Passenger aircraft typically cruise at a high altitude of around 10 km. However, the pressure inside the plane is kept equivalent to an altitude of around 2 km.

Explain why this is necessary.

_____

_____

P3.4 Pressure in liquids

A Liquids, such as water, exert _____ _____ because of how the particles push against each other and anything they touch. There is a difference in _____ between the top and bottom of an object which is in water. This causes a force called _____. This is what causes people to float when they are swimming. When liquids are squeezed their _____ hardly changes at all: they are _____.

B Complete each diagram to show the forces on each object.

   a A boat floating.

           water

   b An anchor about to sink.

           water

C Water pressure is very different deep in the ocean compared to near the surface. Explain how and why it is different, using each of these keywords at least once: **pressure, deeper, weight**

_____

_____

_____

_____

D Freediving is a sport where people dive as deep as they can in the sea on one breath of air. It is dangerous, partly because how well someone can float changes with their depth in the sea.

   a Suggest and explain whether a diver will sink or float at the surface with lungs full of air.

_____

_____

   b When a diver goes below 15 m, they will sink even if they have lungs that are full of air. Use your knowledge of pressure to explain why this is.

_____

_____

_____

E The speed at which water flows from a tap depends on the water pressure in the pipes. Towns, particularly in flatter parts of the world, often build a water tower to help, storing a substantial amount of water 40 m above the ground.

Use your scientific knowledge to explain why a tower helps solve this problem.

_____

_____

P3.5 Pressure on solids

A _____ is defined and calculated as the _____ applied (N) divided by the _____ _____ over which it is applied (m²). It has the unit _____ _____ _____ _____, symbol N/m². If a _____ of one newton is applied over one square metre, there is a _____ of 1 N/m². A _____ force exerted on a _____ area exerts a large _____ on the surface, whereas the same force spread over a _____ area will result in _____ pressure on the surface.

B Recall the formula for calculating pressure for use in this activity.

   a A box of cereal has a weight of 5.0 N, and an area of 0.010 m².
      Calculate the pressure it exerts on its kitchen shelf.

   b A garden shed and its foundations have a weight of 2500 N, and an area of 6.4 m².
      Calculate the pressure between it and the ground.

C Bobby is skiing across country. To avoid sinking into the snow, the pressure under his skis should not exceed 2800 N/m². He has a mass of 78 kg.

   a Calculate Bobby's weight. The gravitational field strength is 10 N/kg.

   b Recall the formula for pressure and rearrange it to calculate the minimum area required for his skis.

D **a** The Canadian lynx and the bobcat are related species of large cat that live in North America. They are both of a similar size and body mass. The lynx lives where there is often deep snow in winter and the bobcat lives where there is little snow.

      Suggest why the lynx has much larger paws than the bobcat.

   b A drawing pin (or thumb tack) has a sharp point, and a large head to make it easier to push the pin into a surface.

      Explain why the point needs to be sharp but the head needs to be large.

P3.6 Turning forces

A When we apply a force to a door that can _____ on its hinges, there is a turning effect called a _____. The _____ of a force is defined and calculated as the _____ applied (N) times the perpendicular _____ to the _____ (m). It has the unit _____ _____, symbol (N m). If a _____ of one newton is applied one metre from a _____, then there is a _____ of one N m. If the sum of the moments in a clockwise direction are equal to the sum of the moments in the anticlockwise direction, the object is in _____ and it will not start turning. This is the _____ _____ _____. The centre of gravity is the point through which the _____ appears to act. If the centre of gravity of an object is directly _____ or _____ the pivot, there will be _____ moment making it turn. If it is to the side of the pivot, the object will start to _____ due to the moment.

B Recall the formula for calculating moment of force for use in this activity.

   a Callum applies 5.0 N of force to a door handle 0.50 m from the hinges to open the door. Calculate the moment of force.

      _____

   b Molly holds a 50 N bag of groceries. Her forearm is 0.40 m from her elbow to her hand. Calculate the moment of force of the groceries about her elbow.

      _____

   c Tightrope walkers must keep their centre of gravity directly above the rope. Explain why this is important.

      _____

      _____

      _____

C Fatima is trying to open a jar of jam. She has a problem with her hand and can only grip with a force of 150 N.

To help her open jars she uses a tool with a handle, such that the radius to the middle of her hand is increased to 110 mm.

The jar requires a moment of 10 N m to open it.

   a Rearrange the formula for calculating moment so that you can calculate force.

   b **i** Calculate the minimum force required to open the jar using the tool.

        _____

      ii Suggest whether she can now open it and why.

        _____

Pinchpoint question

Answer the question below, then do the follow-up activity **with the same letter** as the answer you picked.

Daisy is riding a bicycle down a straight road. This is the distance–time graph for her journey.

Choose the option below that correctly describes her motion at the specified time.

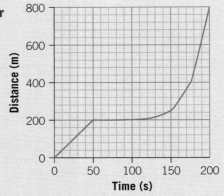

	Time range	Motion
A	From 0 s to 50 s	Daisy is stationary
B	From 100 s to 200 s	Daisy is accelerating and has constant speed
C	From 0 s to 200 s	Daisy has an average speed of 4.0 m/s
D	From 0 s to 50 s	Daisy is accelerating

Follow-up activities

A a Complete the sentences using these keywords.

no	distance travelled	time taken	zero	horizontal (level)

Speed is _____ _____ divided by the _____ _____.

If someone travels _____ distance because they are stationary, their speed is _____.

On a distance–time graph, no change in distance means that the graph will not go higher or lower, it will stay

_____.

b On these axes, sketch a graph to show Daisy:

i stationary

Distance

Time

ii moving with increasing speed

Distance

Time

Hint: What does the slope of a distance–time graph tell us? See P2 3.2 Motion graphs for help.

B a Complete the sentences using these keywords.

steep   curve   slope   changing   shallow   speed

The _____ of a distance–time graph shows the _____ of the object. A fast object

is shown with a _____ line, a slow one with a _____ line. If Daisy is cycling in

a straight line and accelerating, then her speed must be _____, so the slope of the line must

_____ upwards.

b On these axes, sketch a graph to show Daisy moving with:

    i **slow** constant speed   **ii** **fast** constant speed   **iii** increasing speed

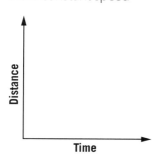 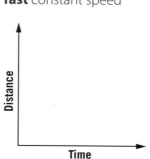 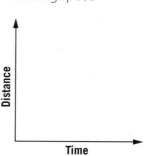

Hint: What does the slope of a distance–time graph tell us? See P2 3.2 Motion graphs for help.

C Balanced forces mean that an object is in equilibrium and its speed is not changing.
Circle the part of Daisy's journey that matches each force diagram.

a 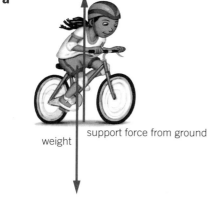   **b**    **c**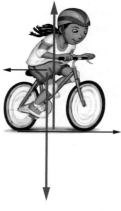

0 s to 50 s / 50 s to 100 s /   **0 s to 50 s / 50 s to 100 s /**   **0 s to 50 s / 50 s to 100 s /**
100 s to 200 s   **100 s to 200 s**   **100 s to 200 s**

Hint: How do unbalanced forces affect an object? See P1 1.5 Balanced and unbalanced for help.

D a Circle the correct **bold** word in each sentence.

To start moving, **unbalanced / balanced** forces are needed to cause Daisy to accelerate. Acceleration means her speed must **change / stay constant**. Once Daisy is moving, the acceleration can drop to zero while she continues moving with **increasing / constant** speed. On a distance–time graph, a straight line with constant slope shows **increasing / constant** speed, which means that she **can / cannot** be accelerating.

Hint: What is acceleration? See P2 3.2 Motion graphs for help.

b Sketch a graph on the axes given to show different parts of a journey in a car, where the car is:

    i   accelerating
    ii moving at a constant speed
    iii stationary

c Which of the sections of your graph show balanced forces? _____

 Pinchpoint review

Now look back at the question – do you think you chose the right letter?
Turn to the Answers page to find out.

P2 Revision questions

1 a Circle the quantity that flows in an electric circuit. *(1 mark)*

resistance   potential difference

charge   components

b When a potential difference of 12 V is applied across a bulb, a current of 4.0 A flows through it. Calculate the resistance of the bulb. Give the unit.

The formula for calculating resistance is:

$$\text{resistance} = \frac{\text{potential difference}}{\text{current}}$$ *(2 marks)*

_____

c The wires leading into the bulb are wrapped with plastic with a resistance of 1 000 000 Ω. Circle whether the plastic wrapping and the filament wire are conductors or insulators.

filament wire: **conductor / insulator** *(1 mark)*

plastic wrapping: **conductor / insulator** *(1 mark)*

2 An engineer is designing a machine to lift patients in a hospital.

a The machine must increase the gravitational potential energy store for the patient by at least 1200 J in 20 s.

Calculate the minimum power needed from the motor and include the unit for power. The formula for calculating power is:

$$\text{power} = \frac{\text{energy}}{\text{time}}$$ *(2 marks)*

_____

b For convenience, the engineer decides to use a rechargeable battery. The hospital managers need to know how much it will cost to charge the battery. The battery recharges at 60 W for 2 hours, and the electricity company charges 15p per kW h.

i Convert 60 W to kW. *(1 mark)*

_____

ii Calculate the cost of charging the battery for 2 hours. Give your answer in pence. *(3 marks)*

_____

3 a **Figure 1** shows a distance–time graph for one part of a journey.

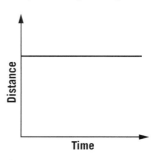

Figure 1

Describe what is happening. *(1 mark)*

_____

b **Table 1** contains data for Clara walking to visit a friend.

Table 1

Time (s)	Distance (m)
0	0
120	180
180	180
300	280

Draw a distance–time graph for this journey. *(3 marks)*

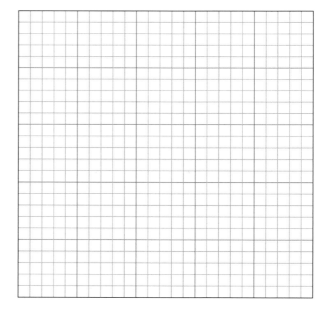

c Calculate the speed of the first part of Clara's journey. *(3 marks)*

_____

4 🔬🔬 In 2006, Hannah McKeand set the record for reaching the South Pole in the fastest time.

a In one hour she travelled approximately 3000 m pulling a sledge of food and equipment requiring a force of about 200 N.

Calculate the work she did in one hour and give the unit of work. *(2 marks)*

_____

b On her trip, McKeand needed to absorb 3000 kJ of energy from her food each hour. While working in an office, a typical adult would need to consume 400 kJ of energy in her food every hour.

Is McKeand's energy intake larger or smaller than that of an office worker? Suggest why. *(2 marks)*

_____

_____

5 🔬🔬 The pressure of a gas is important; for instance, air pressure helps us to predict the weather.

a Tick the variables that affect the pressure of a gas.
(2 marks)

1	temperature	☐
2	electrical charge	☐
3	volume	☐
4	distance	☐

b Give the formula for calculating pressure. *(1 mark)*

_____

c Sometimes people get stuck in thick mud by rivers. A problem for firefighters when they rescue them is avoiding get stuck themselves. A firefighter has a large board to stand on, which measures 1.8 m long and 0.50 m wide.

i Calculate the area of the board. *(1 mark)*

_____

ii The firefighter has a weight of 800 N. Calculate the pressure he will exert when standing on the board and include the unit. *(2 marks)*

_____

iii If the pressure on the ground is above 20 000 N/m², the firefighter will sink into the mud. Explain whether he will sink if he stands on the board. *(1 mark)*

_____

6 🔬🔬🔬 A gravitational field causes a ball to fall, and an electric field causes an electron to accelerate in a circuit. Tick which statements are true for each type of field. *(5 marks)*

Statement	Gravitational	Electric
Becomes weaker with distance		
Object must have mass to be affected by field		
Object must have charge to be affected by field		
Can attract		
Can repel		

7 🔬🔬🔬 Finn is investigating electromagnets. For each change he makes to an electromagnet, circle the effect it will have on the electromagnet's strength and give a reason.

a An increase in current makes the strength **decrease / stay the same / increase** because
(2 marks)

_____

b A decrease in the number of turns on the coil makes the strength **decrease / stay the same / increase** because *(2 marks)*

_____

8 🔬🔬🔬 Explain whether each of the following materials is a thermal insulator or conductor and why.

a Copper *(2 marks)*

_____

_____

b Expanded polystyrene *(2 marks)*

_____

_____

9 🧪🧪🧪 You are a scientific adviser to the British Government. They have asked for advice on future electricity generation.

Discuss the advantages and disadvantages of the two energy resources shown in **Table 2**. *(6 marks)*

Table 2

Energy resource	Estimated cost per unit of electricity in 2015 (£ / MW h)
Natural gas	74
Onshore wind	89

_____

_____

_____

_____

_____

_____

_____

10 🧪🧪🧪 Ezra has a 1500 W kettle and is deciding whether to buy a new 3000 W kettle.
Using the information in **Table 3**, predict and explain whether Ezra's electricity bill is likely to increase, decrease, or stay the same. *(4 marks)*

Table 3

Kettle power (W)	Time to boil 1 kg of water (s)
1500	300
3000	140

_____

_____

_____

_____

_____

_____

11 🧪🧪🧪 **a** Male stag beetles have jaws 30 mm long and a strong bite of 8.0 N.

Calculate the moment of force and include the units. Work in metres. The formula for moment of force is:

moment = force × distance from pivot *(2 marks)*

b Scissors are a type of lever.

When using scissors, it is easier to cut when the object is nearer to the pivot rather than at the end of the blade.

pivot

Figure 2

Explain why using the concept of moments. *(4 marks)*

_____

_____

_____

_____

_____

_____

_____

12 🧪🧪🧪 Leah is a biologist working with animals that live very deep in the ocean. She has heard that animals can be harmed when they are brought up to the surface.

For each hypothesis below, give whether each cause is correct or not and a reason for your answer. *(6 marks)*

a "Water in animal's body expanding" is **correct / incorrect** because

_____

_____

b "Large increase in pressure" is **correct / incorrect** because

_____

_____

c "Large decrease in pressure" is **correct / incorrect** because

_____

_____

P2 Checklist

Revision question number	Outcome	Topic reference	☹	😐	😊
1a	Name what flows in a circuit.	P2 1.2			
1b	Calculate resistance of a component and of a circuit.	P2 1.5			
1c	Describe the difference between conductors and insulators in terms of resistance.	P2 1.5			
2a, b, c	Predict the power requirements of different equipment and how much it costs to use.	P2 2.7			
3a	Calculate work done.	P2 2.8			
3b	Interpret data on food intake for some activities.	P2 2.1			
4a, b, c, d	Interpret distance–time graphs.	P2 3.2			
5a	State two things that can affect gas pressure.	P2 3.3			
5b	State the equation of pressure.	P2 3.5			
5c, d, e	Calculate pressure.	P2 3.5			
6	Compare a gravitational field and an electric field.	P2 1.1			
7	Predict the effect of changes made to an electromagnet, using scientific knowledge to justify the claim.	P2 1.7			
8	Explain why certain materials are good insulators.	P2 2.4			
9	Compare the advantages and disadvantages of using renewable and non-renewable energy resources.	P2 2.6			
10	Predict the effect on energy bills of changing the power of equipment.	P2 2.7			
11 a	Calculate the moment of a force.	P2 3.6			
11b	Apply the concept of moments to everyday situations.	P2 3.6			
12	Predict how water pressure changes in an unfamiliar context.	P2 3.4			

Answers

B1.1

A balanced, nutrients, carbohydrates, lipids, proteins, vitamins, minerals, fibre

B carbohydrate – main source of energy; lipid – store of energy / keep you warm / protect organs: protein – growth and repair of body tissues; vitamins and minerals – keep you healthy

C adds bulk to your food, which keeps it moving through intestines; waste is pushed out of the body more easily / prevents constipation

D baked beans – more fibre / less salt / less fat (less carbohydrate – depending on the person's energy requirements)

B1.2

A food tests, iodine, starch, red, purple, protein, cloudy

B starch – iodine; lipid – ethanol; simple sugar – Benedict's solution; protein – copper sulfate and sodium hydroxide (Biuret solution)

C rub on filter / greaseproof / brown paper, hold up to the light, goes translucent

D **a** **X** and **Y** **b** **Y** and **Z** **c** sugar and lipids

 d sample **Y** – animal products do not contain starch / milk contains lipids, sugar (lactose), and protein

 e e.g. possible allergies / presence of lipids / sugar may not be wanted if on a calorie-controlled diet

B1.3

A malnourishment, underweight, deficiency, starvation, fat, obese

B tiredness / poor immune system / lack of energy / (named) vitamin deficiency

C diabetes / heart disease / stroke / some cancers

D **a** **i** 15 000 – 10 000 = 5000 kJ

 ii more labour-intensive profession so more energy is required for movement / use of muscles

 b **i** 11 000 – 9000 = 2000; $\frac{2000}{11\,000} \times 100 = 22.2\%$

 ii extra energy required to support growing baby

E if you take in more energy that you use (through eating too much food, or too much fatty food) you gain body mass; this is stored as fat under the skin and can result in obesity

B1.4

A digestive system, gullet, stomach, acids, digestion, small, large, rectum, anus

B clockwise from top: gullet, stomach, large intestine, rectum, small intestine

C stomach – where food is mixed with digestive juices and acids; large intestine – water reabsorbed, only solid undigested food / faeces remain

D thin wall – to speed up diffusion / absorption; covered in villi – increase surface area; rich blood supply – carry away absorbed food molecules (maintain diffusion gradient)

E large food molecules are broken into small molecules; these can be absorbed through the wall of the small intestine and transported in blood to where needed in the body

B1.5

A bacteria, vitamins, enzymes, catalyst, carbohydrase, sugar, protease, protein, lipase, glycerol, bile

B **a** **X** and **Y** **b** Enzymes are made of proteins. Enzymes are not used up during a reaction

C *carbohydrase* – carbohydrate – sugars; lipase – *lipid* – fatty acids and glycerol; protease – protein – *amino acids*

D **a** large intestine **b** fibre

 c make vitamins such as vitamin K which are absorbed by the body to keep you healthy

B1.6

A drugs, recreational, medicinal, addiction, withdrawal symptoms

B **a** taken to benefit health / cure diseases / treat symptoms – e.g. antibiotic / paracetamol / aspirin

 b taken for enjoyment / have no health benefit – e.g. ecstasy / caffeine / alcohol / tobacco

C **a** liver / brain **b** lung / mouth **c** speeds up

D **a** to kill bacteria / treat bacterial infection

 b to relieve pain

E withdrawal symptoms make stopping harder / socially withdrawn / increased crime for money / infection spread through needles

B1.7

A ethanol, nervous, depressant, liver, unit, alcoholic(s)

B **a** liver, brain

 b between 1991 and 2008, the number of alcohol-related deaths has increased from 9 per 100 000 of the population to 19 per 100 000 of the population

C **a** alcohol reduces sperm production, so decreases likelihood of conception

 b diffuses into baby's blood damaging organs and nervous system causing FAS / learning difficulties / still or premature birth

B1.8

A cancer / disease, heart, passive, airways, monoxide, oxygen, stimulant, miscarriage

B **a** sticky black material that collects in lungs and contains chemicals that can cause cancer

 b gas that binds to red blood cells, stopping them from carrying as much oxygen

 c stimulant that speeds up the nervous system / makes heart beat faster / narrows blood vessels

C the more cigarettes smoked, the greater the risk of lung cancer (does not mean you will get disease); approximately linear correlation

D chemicals in tobacco smoke stop cilia moving, so mucus containing dirt and microorganisms flows more freely into the lungs where microorganisms can cause an infection

E increases risk of miscarriage / low birth weight and affects fetal development

B2 Chapter 1 Pinchpoint

A this is an incorrect answer – **muscles** in the wall of the intestine move the food along the gut

B this is an incorrect answer – digestion **and** absorption are carried out in the small intestine

C this is the correct answer

D this is an incorrect answer – the wall of the small intestine is **not** smooth, it is covered in villi

Pinchpoint follow-up

A fibre, bulk, muscles, wall, push against, squeezing a tube of toothpaste, soluble, small, speeds up, feces, rectum

B **a** carbohydrates into sugar molecules, proteins into amino acids, lipids into fatty acids and glycerol

 b mouth – carbohydrase, stomach – carbohydrase, protease, small intestine – carbohydrase, protease, lipase

C **a** carbohydrates

 b reduced surface area for absorption; reduction in absorption of digested food particles; person malnourished / suffers from a deficiency causing e.g. tiredness, named deficiency condition (calcium / iron / B_{12})

D **a** **i** 3 **ii** 1 **iii** 2

 b ensures that the blood always has a lower concentration of a food molecule than the intestine so digested food molecules diffuse down concentration gradient / from high to low concentration

B2.1

A algae, producers, photosynthesis, consumers, water, glucose, chlorophyll

B **a** water, light, oxygen   **b** glucose and oxygen
    c carbon dioxide and water

C **a** 5, 4, 2, 7, 1, 6, 3   **b** iodine will turn blue-black

D **a** diffuses through tiny holes / stomata on underside of leaf
    b diffuses into root hair cells from soil
    c absorbed by chlorophyll in chloroplasts

E the greater the rate of producer photosynthesis, the greater the biomass increase; more food available for primary consumer; more organisms available for next level of food chain

B2.2

A leaves, stomata, carbon dioxide, oxygen, veins, palisade, chloroplasts

B clockwise from top-left – waxy layer, chloroplast, palisade layer, spongy layer, air space, guard cell, stoma

C **a** transport water and glucose to cells in leaf
    b reduces water loss through evaporation
    c open and close stomata
    d allow gases to diffuse into and out of leaf

D most chloroplasts found in the top of leaf in palisade layer as this is the area of the leaf which receives most sunlight; this therefore maximises amount of sunlight absorbed by chlorophyll in chloroplasts, maximising photosynthesis

E thin – allows carbon dioxide to diffuse in to maximise photosynthesis (and oxygen to diffuse out); large surface area maximises the amount of sunlight which can be absorbed to maximise photosynthesis

B2.3

A minerals, magnesium, potassium, nitrates, phosphates, deficiency, fertilisers

B nitrate – healthy growth – poor growth, older leaves are yellowed; phosphate – healthy roots – poor root growth, younger leaves look purple; potassium – healthy leaves and flowers – yellow leaves with dead patches; magnesium – making chlorophyll – plant leaves turn yellow

C **a** magnesium   **b** chlorophyll, which makes a plant green, contains magnesium, so if a plant has a magnesium deficiency it won't produce much / any chlorophyll, so leaves are not green

D **a** 31 cm   **b** no: results are too similar for B and C; the scientist would need to look for other symptoms such as purple leaves to distinguish which seedlings were grown in the dummy supplement

B2.4

A bacteria, chemosynthesis, chemical, glucose, sulfur, sea

B chemical; glucose; carbon dioxide

C sulfur bacteria found near volcanic vents at the bottom of the sea use hydrogen sulfide; nitrogen bacteria found in plant roots and soil use nitrogen compounds

D chemosynthesis – chemical, sometimes, sometimes, yes; photosynthesis – light, yes, yes, yes

E tubeworms have no stomach; sulfur bacteria live inside the tubeworm and use chemicals from the tubeworm to make food; the tubeworms then feed off the substances made by the bacteria; both organisms benefit

B2.5

A aerobic respiration, glucose, mitochondria, water, carbohydrates, plasma, diffuses haemoglobin

B oxygen, carbon dioxide

C **a** mitochondria
    b need to transfer lots of energy to contract (to effect movement)

D **a** **i** number of repeats of named exercise / activity
       ii breathing rate / number of breaths in named time
       iii length of activity
    b as exercise level increases, breathing rate increases as more oxygen needs to be taken to cells for respiration, to transfer more energy for movement

E **a** food is broken down during digestion releasing glucose; glucose absorbed through wall of small intestine into blood stream where it dissolves into plasma; carried around the body and diffuses into cells that need it
    b during inhalation, oxygen enters the lungs and diffuses into blood stream through alveoli; oxygen joins to haemoglobin in red blood cells and is carried around the body; it then diffuses into the cells that need it

B2.6

A anaerobic respiration, lactic acid, oxygen debt, fermentation, ethanol

B glucose → lactic acid

C aerobic: glucose is a reactant; oxygen is a reactant; carbon dioxide is produced; water is produced; anaerobic: glucose is a reactant; lactic acid is produced

D **a** aerobic respiration transfers more energy per glucose molecule, anaerobic respiration can cause painful muscle cramps
    b when they require a lot of energy quickly, e.g. to escape from danger

E **a** fermentation
    b yeast ferments sugar in barley grains producing alcohol
    c yeast ferments sugars / carbohydrates in flour into ethanol and carbon dioxide; the gas makes dough rise and ethanol evaporates during cooking

B2.7

A food chain, energy, producer, photosynthesis, consumers, prey, predator, food web, linked / interconnected

B food chain shows the transfer or energy between organisms; food web shows linked food chains

C **a** food chain beginning with the dandelion then 3 correct links, e.g. dandelion → grasshopper → spider → owl
    b producer: dandelion; herbivore: beetle / grasshopper / slug; carnivore: shrew / spider / mouse / owl; predator: shrew / spider / mouse / owl; prey: shrew / spider / mouse

D as energy is transferred along the food chain, much is transferred to the surroundings by heating and waste products; therefore, less energy is available at each level in a food chain

B2.8

A interdependence, population, increase, bioaccumulation

B very small amounts of mercury enter plankton; fish eat many plankton; mercury accumulates (bioaccumulation) but level still safe for humans; shark eat many fish; mercury accumulates to a level that is toxic

C initially lionfish ate many native fish so lionfish population increased and native fish population decreased; eventually not enough food for lionfish so their population decreased; fewer native fish now eaten so their population increases, more food now available for lionfish so cycle starts again

D wolf population eats the elk population, decreasing their numbers; this means less willow is eaten by elks so more is available for the beavers; the beavers use willow to make dams which affects the water flow in rivers and streams

B2.9

A habitat, community, ecosystem, co-exist, niche

B **a** food sources / niches; parts of the tree

b habitat: oak tree; community: birds, ants, squirrels, woodlice, slugs, and oak tree

C **a** **i** quadrat   **ii** hedgerow

b more light / water / space further from the hedgerow

c you have not chosen where to place the quadrat, e.g. an interesting area – sample locations were selected before starting

B2 Chapter 2 Pinchpoint

A this is an incorrect answer – this is the word equation for **aerobic respiration**

B this is an incorrect answer – plants **do not** breathe as they do not have lungs; gas exchange occurs in the leaf

C this is an incorrect answer – minerals are **not** needed for photosynthesis but do help a plant to remain healthy

D this is the correct answer

Pinchpoint follow-up

A **a** carbon dioxide and water underlined

b glucose and oxygen circled

c carbon dioxide + water $\xrightarrow{\text{light}}$ glucose + oxygen

B leaves, stomata, carbon dioxide, oxygen, photosynthesis, stomata, energy

C **a** dish 4

b water is required for photosynthesis (so both seedlings 2 and 4 remained alive); seedling 4 also had access to minerals from the soil, which are needed for healthy growth

D **a** **three** from: light intensity, carbon dioxide concentration, water availability, temperature

b line graph drawn which rises reaching a plateau after a relative light intensity of 6

c as light intensity increases, the rate of photosynthesis increases until it reaches a maximum at a relative light intensity of 6

d light is required for photosynthesis

e rate of photosynthesis is 9.0, as another factor is now limiting the rate of reaction (accept suggested variable e.g. availability of water)

B3.1

A resources, mates, food, light, minerals, adaptations

B **three** from: light – for photosynthesis; water – for photosynthesis and to keep their cells rigid; space – so roots can absorb enough water and leaves can absorb enough light; minerals––to make chemicals needed for healthy growth

C **a** space **or** mates

b space – to hunt / for shelter; mates – to reproduce

c original population would decrease as it has less food, or moves to a new area to find food / original population not affected if it was the stronger competitor

D waxy layer – prevents water evaporating; fleshy stems – store water; widespread roots – collect water from a large area; spines – small surface area to reduce water loss

B3.2

A environment, leaves, fur / coats, adapted, interdependence, increases, food

B **a** solid line – rabbits; dashed line – foxes   **b** Y, Z

c Y – an increasing fox population means that more rabbits are eaten so rabbit population decreases

Z – as number of rabbits increases, the number of foxes will also increase as they have more food available

C plant – e.g. loses leaves in winter to save energy and fallen leaves provide warmth and protection to base of tree; animal – e.g. migration to warmer climate / somewhere with more food / hibernation / grow thicker fur

D only best adapted organisms will survive, e.g. faster animals, increasing the number of organisms in the species with that characteristic; eventually all members of the species will have the characteristic / organisms that are not well adapted will move or die

B3.3

A species, variation, inherited, environmental

B inherited – eye colour, blood group; environment – accent, pierced ears; combination of both – height, skin colour

C environmental variation is caused by an organism's surroundings whereas inherited variation is caused by the genetic material a person inherits from their parents

D **a** they each inherit a different mixture of genetic material from their parents (inherited variation) so they share some characteristics with each other but not all

b environment now also has an influence on the kittens' appearance, e.g. amount of food eaten (environmental variation) affects the cats' mass

B3.4

A discontinuous, bar chart, continuous, histogram

B continuous – leg length, fish mass, leaf surface area; discontinuous – blood group, flower colour, number of spots

C **a** a characteristic that can take any value within a range

b a characteristic that can only result in certain values

D **a** **i** continuous variation

ii caused by a mixture of inherited variation and environmental variation; the seedling may inherit the ability to be tall but this will only occur if you have nutrient-rich soil / enough light

b histogram

B3.5

A nucleus, DNA, chromosomes, genes

B egg and sperm drawn each containing 23 chromosomes, combining to make a fertilised egg with 46 chromosomes

C a gene holds the information to produce a specific characteristic (or protein) such as eye colour

D Franklin and Wilkins took first image of DNA using X-rays; Watson and Crick saw image and identified that DNA had a helical structure; they then carried out further studies to discover that DNA is a double helix / like a twisted ladder

B3.6

A evolved, millions, natural selection, survive, genes, fossils

B 4, 6, 2, 5, 1, 3

C **a** remains or traces of animals that lived many years ago

b evidence of species that are now extinct, e.g. dinosaurs

D named example, e.g. peppered moth; before industrial revolution, more pale moths, camouflaged against pale bark so survived and reproduced (dark moths seen and eaten); after revolution, dark moths increased as camouflaged against soot on bark; population evolved to be predominantly dark

B3.7

A biodiversity, habitats, disease, extinct, endangered, seed bank

B **a** store genetic samples from different species which could be used in the future for research or to produce new individuals

b **two** from: seed banks – store dried seeds at low temperatures to prevent germination; tissue banks – buds and other plant cells stored for research; cryobanks – gamete cells / embryos /

seeds stored in liquid nitrogen – used to create new organisms (in animals via surrogacy); pollen banks – store pollen grains to fertilise other plants

C **three** from: outbreak of a new disease – organisms killed by a microorganism; introduction of new competitors – lack of food; environmental change – drought; destruction of habitat / deforestation – loss of food / shelter

B2 Chapter 3 Pinchpoint

A this is an incorrect answer – evolution takes place over **many** generations

B this is the correct answer

C this is an incorrect answer – evolution does not **always** take millions of years

D this is an incorrect answer – the organism itself does not change, the characteristic in the **species** changes

Pinchpoint follow-up

A a 0.5% or 1 in 200 b 33% or 1 in 3

  c the proportion of the population with the advantageous characteristic increases over time, as the organisms containing this characteristic are more likely to be able to catch prey and so survive and reproduce passing on their advantageous genes; slower organisms are more likely to die without reproducing (or reproducing as many times)

B a few bacteria in the population have resistance to the antibiotic (through a mutation); these survive and reproduce, passing on the gene to the next generation; bacteria without gene are killed; number of resistant bacteria in population increases; after many generations, all bacteria in population have antibiotic resistance

C a pale, camouflaged, dark, eaten, pale, reproduced, soot, dark, camouflaged, decreasing, increasing, dark

  b 47 (occurred quickly as moths have a very short life cycle)

D e.g. 1 – a number of short- and long-necked giraffes; 2 – long-necked giraffes reaching leaves, short-necked giraffes not able to reach; 3 – only long-necked giraffes alive (short-necked giraffes may be drawn dead); 4 – sperm and egg joining together / chromosome with a gene identified; 5 – all long-necked giraffes

B2 Revision Questions

1 a i reduce water evaporation [1]
    ii stops cactus being eaten [1]
    iii collect water from a large area [1]
  b i loses leaves / enters dormant phase [1]
    ii hibernation / migration / grow thick fur [1]

2 a increase [1] b decrease [1]
  c toxic chemical taken into thrush when it eats snails [1]; chemical taken into body of hawk when thrushes eaten [1]; as hawks eat many thrushes, level becomes so high it kills / bioaccumulation [1]

3 a protein – to repair body tissues and make new cells; carbohydrates – main source of energy; lipids – to provide a store of energy, insulation and protect organs [2 for all correct, 1 for 1 correct]
  b adds bulk to food [1] to keep it moving through intestine / help waste be pushed out of body / prevent constipation [1]
  c $\frac{2520}{8400} \times 100$ [1] = 30% [1]
  d add Benedict's solution [1], heat (in water bath) [1]; if solution turns orange-red it contains sugar [1]

4 a i carbohydrase / amylase [1]
    ii breaks down carbohydrates / starch [1] into glucose / sugar molecules [1]
  b speed up reactions [1] without being used up [1]
  c live on fibre in the intestines [1]; make vitamins / vitamin K [1]

5 a i oxygen [1], water [1] ii mitochondria [1]
  b **two** from: anaerobic doesn't need oxygen, aerobic does [1]; anaerobic produces lactic acid, aerobic does not [1]; aerobic transfers more energy per glucose molecule [1]; aerobic produces carbon dioxide and water, anaerobic does not [1]
  c i fermentation (anaerobic respiration in yeast) [1]
    ii microorganism / yeast [1]

6 a i e.g. hair colour, ear piercing [1]
    ii e.g. eye colour, blood group, attached / free-hanging earlobes [1]
  b i number of spikes labelled on x-axis and frequency on y-axis [1]; appropriate scale used [1]; 3 data points plotted correctly [1]; all data points plotted correctly [1]
    ii 10 [1]
  c i discontinuous [1]
    ii more light allows more photosynthesis [1]; leaves grow bigger [1] so could have more spikes [1]

7 a **one** resource and **one** reason from: water [1] – for photosynthesis / to stay upright [1]; space [1] – to collect light / water / minerals [1]; minerals [1] – for healthy growth [1]
  b animals cannot photosynthesise to make food [1], and have to gain energy by eating other organisms [1]
  c **six** from: organisms in prey species show variation [1]; those most adapted survive **and** reproduce [1]; named adaptation, e.g. fastest [1]; less well-adapted die [1]; genes from most-adapted individuals are passed onto next generation [1]; offspring are likely to display the advantageous characteristic / advantageous characteristic becomes more common [1]; reference to natural selection [1]; process repeated over many generations [1]; over time can lead to the development of a new species [1]

8 a medical drugs treat symptoms / cure disease [1]; recreational drugs have no medical benefit / are taken for enjoyment [1]
  b i ethanol (alcohol) [1]
    ii causes liver disease / liver cirrhosis [1], brain damage / stomach ulcers [1], heart disease [1]
  c i blocks arteries [1]; prevents blood flowing to heart – heart attack / brain – stroke [1]
    ii 320 deaths per 100 000 [1]
    iii 1% or 1.025% [2; allow $\frac{1025}{100\,0000} \times 100$ for 1]

9 a place a leaf in boiling water (to break cell walls / soften leaf) [1]; place leaf in ethanol to remove chlorophyll [1]; place on a white tile and add iodine [1]
  b i green part of leaf shaded [1]
    ii photosynthesis can only occur in the green part of the leaf [1] as chlorophyll is needed to absorb light [1]; photosynthesis produces glucose / sugar [1]

10 a similarity – both produce glucose / both need energy / both normally produce carbon dioxide [1]; difference – photosynthesis uses light, chemosynthesis uses chemical / water not always required for chemosynthesis [1]
  b i sulfur bacteria and tubeworms / nitrogen bacteria living in plant root (nodules) [1]
    ii named bacterial benefit, e.g. bacteria use chemicals from tube worms to make food [1]; named organism benefit, e.g. tubeworms live off glucose produced by bacteria [1]

11 a the rabbit offspring inherit half the genetic material from the mother and half from their father [1]
  b i 22 [1]   ii 44 [1]

12 a found in nucleus [1]; all genetic material is made up of the chemical DNA [1], arranged in long strands called chromosomes [1]; short sections of DNA called genes each code for a single characteristic [1]

b Franklin and Wilkins [1] took an X-ray of DNA [1], which was then seen by Watson and Crick [1] who worked out DNA is a double helix structure [1]

C1.1

A non-metals, left, right, high, good, sonorous, physical, chemical

B a J and K

b J has high melting and boiling points, as do most metals; its oxide is basic, as are the oxides of metals

C a **two** from: boron, B; silicon, Si; gallium, Ga; arsenic, As; antimony, Sb; tellurium, Te

b similarities – hard, high melting point, shiny, fairly high density, oxide has high melting point;
differences – semiconductor of electricity (metals are good conductors); brittle (most metals are not brittle)

C1.2

A groups, periods, groups, periods, group / period

B a $\text{density} = \dfrac{\text{mass}}{\text{volume}} = \dfrac{56.6\,\text{g}}{5.0\,\text{cm}^3} = 11.3\,\text{g/cm}^3$

b density increases from top to bottom of both groups; the patterns for both groups are similar

C a in Period 4, melting point increases from left to right for elements in first two groups, and then decreases; in Period 5, melting point increases from left to right for elements in first three groups, and then decreases

b melting point – greater than 1850 °C and less than 3000 °C (actual value is 2220 °C); reason – if patterns in Periods 5 and 6 are the same, Hf has a lower melting point than Ta; if patterns in all groups shown are the same, Hf has a greater melting point than Zr

C1.3

A left, conduct, low, reactive, two / new, hydrogen, hydroxide

B a for each element, boiling point is greater than melting point; both melting point and boiling point decrease from top to bottom of the group

b any value below 39 °C (actual value is 29 °C)

C a white solid **b** $2\text{Li} + \text{Cl}_2 \rightarrow 2\text{LiCl}$ **c** caesium chloride

C1.4

A right, halogens, metals, reactions

B top symbol – corrosive, burns eyes, wear eye protection; lower symbol – toxic, difficulty breathing, use fume cupboard

C top row: **V**, **X**; middle row: **Y**, **W**; bottom row: **Y**, **Y**

D a first row – reaction occurs:
chlorine + potassium iodide → potassium chloride + iodine;
second row – reaction occurs:
fluorine + potassium chloride → potassium fluoride + chlorine;
third and fourth rows – no reaction

b a more reactive halogen (e.g. fluorine) displaces a less reactive halogen (e.g. chlorine) from a solution of its salt (e.g. potassium chloride)

C1.5

A right, noble, metals, unreactive (inert)

B a 3 **b** 3 **c** 1 **d** 2

b all group 0 elements unreactive; reactivity increases from top to bottom of group

C a increases from top to bottom

b any value between −189 °C and −112 °C (actual value is −157 °C); trend shows that melting point increases from top to bottom, so value for krypton is likely to be between the values of the elements immediately above and below it in the group

D group 1 – boiling points decrease from top to bottom of group and all boiling points are above 0 °C; group 0 – boiling points increase from top to bottom of group and all boiling points are below 0 °C

C2 Chapter 1 Pinchpoint

A this is an incorrect answer – the Group 7 element on its own (bromine) is **less reactive** than the one in the compound (fluorine) so no displacement reaction occurs

B this is the correct answer

C this is an incorrect answer – only occurs if the element on its own (bromine) is **more** reactive than the element in the compound (chlorine); bromine is **less** reactive than chlorine, so no reaction occurs

D this is an incorrect answer – chlorine is below fluorine in Group 7, so chlorine is **less** reactive than fluorine; a displacement reaction can only occur if the element on its own is **more** reactive than the element in the compound

Pinchpoint follow-up

A a bromine, fluorine, chlorine, chlorine

b i fluorine and potassium chloride; chlorine and potassium iodide; bromine and potassium iodide

ii fluorine + potassium chloride →
potassium fluoride + chlorine
chlorine + potassium iodide →
potassium chloride + iodine
bromine + potassium iodide →
potassium bromide + iodine

B a fluorine and potassium chloride, chlorine and potassium iodide, fluorine and potassium bromide

b $\text{F}_2 + 2\text{KCl} \rightarrow 2\text{KF} + \text{Cl}_2$; $\text{Cl}_2 + 2\text{KI} \rightarrow 2\text{KCl} + \text{I}_2$;
$\text{F}_2 + 2\text{KBr} \rightarrow 2\text{KF} + \text{Br}_2$

C A displacement reaction occurs between a pair of substances if the **more** reactive Group 7 element is on its own, and if the **less** reactive Group 7 element is part of a compound.
Fluorine is more reactive than chlorine. This means that fluorine and potassium **do** react together in a displacement reaction.
Iodine is **less** reactive than bromine. This means that potassium iodide and bromine react together in a **displacement** reaction. The products are iodine and potassium **bromide**.

D a fluorine, chlorine, bromine, iodine

b 1, 4, 5, 6, 7, 8

C2.1

A pure, sharp, impure, temperatures, more, not, mixture, properties / melting points

B pure substances – X and Z; reason – their melting points are sharp / they do not melt over a range of temperatures

C a i S **ii** P **iii** R **iv** Q

b diagram showing two types of particle, each made up of two or more types of atom (circles of different colours / with different shading)

D sand and water – filtration – sand does not dissolve in water; sand and steel nails – magnet – steel is attracted to magnets, but sand is not; flour and marbles – sieve – each piece of flour is small enough to go through holes in sieve, but marbles are not

C2.2

A solution, solute, solvent, solute, move, cannot, same, liquid, gas

B examples of suitable sentences:
- **a** Sugar dissolves in solvents such as water.
- **b** When you mix sugar and water and stir, sugar is the solute and water is the solvent.
- **c** Sugar dissolves in water to make a solution.

C
- **a** box showing bigger sugar particles surrounded by smaller water particles
- **b** sugar particles separate from each other and spread out; the sugar particles are surrounded by water particles

D
- **a** $1000\,g + 12\,g = 1012\,g$
- **b** $156\,g - 7\,g = 149\,g$
- **c** $1004.6\,g - 9.0\,g = 995.6\,g$

E
- **a** nail polish is soluble in propanone, but not in water
- **b** solvent – water; solutes – carbon dioxide, sugar, flavourings

C2.3

A saturated, solubility, soluble, soluble

B
- **a** A saturated solution contains the **maximum** mass of sugar that will dissolve.
- **b** The solubility of sugar is the mass of sugar that dissolves in $100\,g$ of water to make a **saturated** solution.
- **c** A saturated solution is one in which no more **solute** will dissolve.

C
- **a** 3, 4, 2, 5, 1
- **b** final mass of solution (measured in step 5) minus 100 g

D
- **a** straight line, drawn with a ruler, that passes through, or close to, all the points
- **b** 2, 3

C2.4

A filtering, insoluble, dissolved, liquid, filtrate, residue

B left – residue; right, from top – filter paper cone, filter funnel, clamp, conical flask, filtrate

C 3, 2, 5, 4, 1 **or** 3, 4, 1, 2, 5

D
- **a** **1** – ✓ – pieces of dirt – oil; **2** – ✓ – undissolved potassium chloride – potassium chloride solution; **3** – ✓ – ground-up coffee beans – coffee solution; **4** – ✗
- **b** **one** from: **1** – pieces of dirt / undissolved potassium chloride / ground up coffee beans too big to fit through holes in filter; oil particles / particles in solution small enough to fit through holes

E solubility at $80\,°C = 167\,g/100\,g$ of water and solubility at $20\,°C = 33\,g/100\,g$ of water.
so maximum residue on cooling $= 167\,g - 33\,g = 134\,g$

C2.5

A evaporation, solid, solute, distillation, condensation, solution

B clockwise from top-left: 5, 1, 2, 4, 3

C
- **a** **1** – both; **2** – evaporation; **3** – both; **4** – distillation; **5** – evaporation
- **b** e.g., in both processes, the solvent changes state from liquid to gas; in evaporation, the solvent vapour is not usually collected but in distillation the solvent evaporates, condenses, and is collected

D
- **a** water
- **b** in evaporation, the solvent – in this case water – evaporates and escapes; in order to collect the solvent, the vapour would need to be collected and cooled so that it condenses and can be collected as a liquid

C2.6

A solvent, chromatography, different, spot

B
- **a** 2
- **b** chlorophyll and carotene
- **c** there could be other pigments that travel the same distance up the paper in these conditions
- **d** xanthophyll

C there are no reactants in the reaction mixture, so the reactants must have finished reacting

C2 Chapter 2 Pinchpoint

A this is an incorrect answer – filtration cannot be used to separate dissolved solid from a solution; the technique can only be used to separate undissolved solid that is mixed with a solution

B this is an incorrect answer – the answer is the difference between the solubility at 80 °C and the solubility at 20 °C

C this is an incorrect answer – you cannot use filtration to separate a dissolved substance from its solvent

D this is the correct answer

Pinchpoint follow-up

A 1, 3, 5

B first table, from top: 32, 46, 56, 70
second table, from top: 28, 14, 38, 5

C
- **a** 2
- **b** 1
- **c** 4
- **d** 3
- **e** 3

D
- **a** $2 × 51\,g = 102\,g$
- **b** $100\,g + 46\,g = 146\,g$
- **c** $70\,g - 28\,g = 42\,g$
- **d** mass of solid that dissolves at 70 °C = 61 g; mass of solid that comes out of solution on cooling is 19 g; mass of solid that dissolves at the lower temperature = 61 g – 19 g = 42 g; from the graph, the temperature at which this mass of solid dissolves to make a saturated solution is 30 °C

C3.1

A metals, electricity, hydrogen, magnesium

B
- **a** magnesium – many bubbles quickly formed; zinc – bubbles formed, but fewer than for magnesium; iron – bubbles formed, but slightly fewer than for zinc
- **b** e.g. all the metals react with dilute acid; the reaction with magnesium was most **vigorous**; the reaction with lead was least **vigorous**; this shows that magnesium is the most **reactive** of the four metals; the gas in the bubbles is **hydrogen**

C
- **a** collect the gas; place a lighted splint in the gas; if the splint goes out with a squeaky pop, the gas is hydrogen
- **b** hydrogen + oxygen → water
- **c** $2H_2 + O_2 \rightarrow 2H_2O$

D
- **a** $Mg + H_2SO_4 \rightarrow MgSO_4 + H_2$
- **b** $Mg + 2HCl \rightarrow MgCl_2 + H_2$
- **c** $Zn + H_2SO_4 \rightarrow ZnSO_4 + H_2$
- **d** $Zn + 2HCl \rightarrow ZnCl_2 + H_2$

C3.2

A air, reactive, oxide, oxide, unreactive, state, solid, liquid

B e.g. in the experiment, the metal that burns most vigorously is magnesium – this means that magnesium is the most reactive metal in the experiment; the product of the reaction is magnesium oxide; one metal, copper, does not burn in air – instead, it forms a layer of copper oxide on its surface; copper is less reactive than magnesium, zinc and iron; gold does not react with oxygen at all – it is the least reactive metal in the group

C
- **a** magnesium, zinc, iron, copper, gold
- **b** the metal with the most vigorous reaction is at the top, followed by the metal with the next most vigorous reaction, and so on; gold is at the bottom since it does not react with oxygen when heated in a Bunsen flame

D
- **a** $2Cu(s) + O_2(g) \rightarrow 2CuO(s)$
- **b** $2Mg(s) + O_2(g) \rightarrow 2MgO(s)$
- **c** $2Zn(s) + O_2(g) \rightarrow 2ZnO(s)$
- **d** $4Fe(s) + 3O_2(g) \rightarrow 2Fe_2O_3(s)$

C3.3

A metals, top, unreactive, hydrogen, hydroxides

B **a** magnesium – not vigorous, tiny bubbles formed very slowly – hydrogen – magnesium hydroxide; potassium – very vigorous indeed – hydrogen – potassium hydroxide

   b magnesium reacts very slowly indeed with water, but potassium reacts violently with water; in both cases, one product is hydrogen gas; the reaction of water with magnesium makes magnesium hydroxide solution and the reaction of water with potassium makes potassium hydroxide solution

C **a** put some water in three test tubes; add a different metal to each test tube, and observe what happens

   b the metal that reacts most vigorously is the one closest to the top of the reactivity series, so must be calcium; the one that does not react must be the one closest to the bottom of the reactivity series, i.e. silver; the third metal is then magnesium

C3.4

A more, less, iron oxide, oxide, iron

B **a** Magnesium is **above** copper in the reactivity series.

   b Magnesium is **more** reactive than copper.

   c Magnesium displaces copper from its compound, copper **sulfate**.

   d As the reaction takes place, the colour of the blue copper sulfate solution gets **paler**.

   e As the reaction takes place, the piece of magnesium gets **smaller**.

C 1 – ✗ – copper (the metal on its own) is less reactive than magnesium (the metal in the compound); 2 – ✓ – magnesium (the metal on its own) is more reactive than lead (the metal in the compound); 3 – ✓ – zinc (the metal on its own) is more reactive than lead (the metal in the compound)

D **a** from left: oxygen atom, magnesium atom, copper atom

   b magnesium displaces copper from its compound, copper oxide, to make magnesium oxide and copper

E **a** zinc is more reactive than copper, so it displaces copper from copper sulfate solution; copper appears as a pink-brown solid, and the solution becomes paler as copper sulfate in solution is replaced by zinc sulfate in solution

   b iron, the metal on its own, is less reactive than aluminium, the metal in the compound, and so it cannot displace aluminium from its compounds

C3.5

A crust, mixed, ore, displacement / chemical, displaces, iron

B 2, 1, 3

C zinc – ✓ – zinc is lower in reactivity series than carbon, so can be displaced from its compounds by carbon; magnesium – ✗ – magnesium is higher in reactivity series than carbon, so cannot be displaced from its compounds by carbon; lead – ✓ – lead is lower in reactivity series than carbon, so can be displaced from its compounds by carbon

D **a** $\frac{41}{100} \times 500\,kg = 2050\,kg$

   b $5\,kg = 5000\,g$ $\frac{200\,g}{5000\,g} \times 100 = 4\%$

E **a** lead sulfide + oxygen → lead oxide + sulfur dioxide
   $2PbS + 3O_2 \rightarrow 2PbO + 2SO_2$

   b lead carbonate → lead oxide + carbon dioxide
   $PbCO_3 \rightarrow PbO + CO_2$

   c lead oxide + carbon → lead oxide + carbon dioxide
   $2PbO + C \rightarrow 2Pb + CO_2$

C3.6

A metal, metal, high, insulators, physical, alkalis

B **a** 3   **b** 1   **c** 2

C 1 physical; 2 chemical; 3 physical; 4 physical

D **a** do not conduct electricity, do not react with water

   b **two** from: high melting points, do not react with water, strong when forces press on it

E **a** the ceramic material

   b the position of the masses and the size of the piece of ceramic material

   c to hold the ceramic material firmly in position

   d this 'measuring instrument' has a greater resolution

C3.7

A long, many, many, different, atoms

B **a** it is strong, very flexible, and waterproof

   b nylon is stronger than poly(propene)

   c HDPE and rigid PVC; reasons both are rigid and waterproof

   d both are flexible and waterproof; flexible PVC has a greater strength than LDPE when pulled, by 5 MPa; the density of flexible PVC is (1.30 – 0.92) = 0.38 g/cm^3 greater than the density of LDPE

C polymer **X** is flexible because the molecules can slide over each other; polymer **Y** is rigid because the links that join the long molecules together stop the long molecules sliding over each other

D advantages of wood – renewable, biodegradable, attractive; disadvantage of wood – can be damaged by water (can rot); advantages of HDPE – easy to clean, waterproof; does not rot; disadvantages of HDPE – made from a non-renewable resource (oil); difficult to dispose of since it is non-biodegradable

C3.8

A mixture, different, combination, pushing / squashing, pushing / squashing

B 2, 3

C **a** **i** one that is made up of two or more materials; in this case, rubber and steel

      ii the steel cords make the tyre stronger

   b a building made from concrete alone may be damaged by stretching forces, but a building made from reinforced concrete can withstand stretching forces as a result of the steel, as well as pushing forces as a result of the concrete

D the CFRP bicycle is stronger, and will also be lighter since the material has a lower density; the CFRP bicycle will not rust, but the steel one will

C2 Chapter 3 Pinchpoint

A this is the correct answer

B this is an incorrect answer – only metals that are **less** reactive than carbon can be extracted from their compounds by heating with carbon

C this is an incorrect answer – rubidium and beryllium are above carbon in the reactivity series, which shows that they are **more** reactive than carbon

D this is an incorrect answer – only metals that are **less** reactive than carbon can be extracted from their compounds by heating with carbon

Pinchpoint follow-up

A **a** sodium; $TiCl_4 + 4Na \rightarrow Ti + 4NaCl$

   b aluminium; $Cr_2O_3 + 2Al \rightarrow Al_2O_3 + 2Cr$

   c hydrogen; $WO_3 + 3H_2 \rightarrow W + 3H_2O$

B **a** 4   **b** 5   **c** 3   **d** 6

C **a** most reactive – rubidium; least reactive – nickel

   b most reactive – potassium; least reactive – chromium

   c most reactive – barium; least reactive – copper

   d most reactive – rubidium; least reactive – strontium

   e most reactive – chromium; least reactive – copper

D The reactivity series lists metals in order of reactivity. Metals at the **top** are more reactive than metals at the **bottom**. Carbon is also included

in the reactivity series, even though it is not a metal; If a metal is **below** carbon in the reactivity series, it is less reactive than carbon. A metal that is **less** reactive than carbon may be extracted from its compounds by heating with carbon. A **displacement** reaction occurs. The word equations below show examples of displacement reactions in which a metal is extracted from a compound by heating with **carbon**: tin oxide + carbon → tin ~~oxide~~ + carbon dioxide
lead oxide + carbon ~~dioxide~~ → lead + carbon dioxide

C4.1

A layers, inner, outer, mantle, solid, flow, crust, atmosphere, troposphere, nitrogen, oxygen

B e.g. the outer and inner core are both mainly iron and nickel, but the outer core is liquid and the inner core is solid; the crust, mantle, and inner core are all solid, but they are made of different materials; both the mantle and outer core can flow

C **a** $\dfrac{78}{100} \times 250\,\text{m}^3 = 195\,\text{m}^3$

    b **i** $\dfrac{84}{400} \times 100 = 21\%$

       ii oxygen, because the air is 21% oxygen

D **a** **two** from: the layer on the outside of the Earth is relatively thin; the layer on the outside of Earth and egg is solid; the Earth and egg are made up of separate layers; the layer that is in the very middle is solid

    b **two** from: the egg is egg-shaped but the shape of the Earth is closer to spherical; the Earth has a liquid outer core, which is not shown in the egg model

C4.2

A metamorphic, soft, biological, sediments, transport, deposition, compaction, cementation (either order), compaction, joins, cementation

B 1, 4, 2, 3

C **a** biological – the breaking up or wearing down of rock by the action of living things; chemical – the breaking up or wearing down of a rock by the action of substances, e.g. those in rainwater; physical – the breaking up or wearing down of rock, e.g. because of changing temperature

    b the movement of sediments far from their original rock

D porous – there are gaps between the grain because sedimentary rocks were formed from separate sediments; soft – the forces holding the grains together are not very strong because the sediments were joined together by compaction or cementation

C4.3

A magma, lava, solidifies / freezes, crystals, non-porous, hard, pressure, crystals

B **a** both types of rock consist of crystals

    b igneous rocks are formed when liquid rock freezes; metamorphic rock formation does not involve liquid rock **or** metamorphic rock formation does not involve changes of state **or** metamorphic rock is formed from existing rock as a result of the action of heat or pressure (without melting)

C **a** warm – bigger crystals formed – particles have more time to arrange themselves into crystals; cold – smaller crystals formed – particles have less time to arrange themselves into crystals

    b underground, liquid rock cools more slowly than liquid rock on the surface, so the crystals are bigger in igneous rock formed underground

D not porous – no gaps between crystals – formed from liquid that cools and solidifies; hard – strong forces between particles – formed from liquid that cools and solidifies

C4.4

A recycled, sedimentary, freezes / solidifies, igneous, temperatures / heating, metamorphic, uplift

B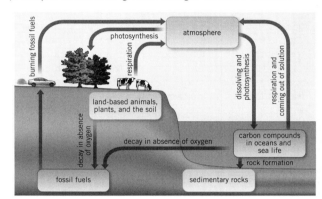

C e.g., plant roots grow in a crack in the rock, eventually forcing small pieces of rock to break off; the sediments are transported in a stream to the sea; the sediments are deposited, and form sedimentary rock by compaction; the sedimentary rock is close to some magma, and warms up; particles in the sediments move, and form crystals of metamorphic rock

C4.5

A reservoirs, sedimentary, fossil, cycle, respire, burn / combust, photosynthesis, dissolving, same, change / increase / decrease

B

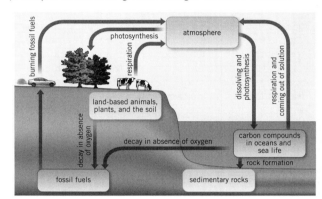

C **a** carbon dioxide was added to the atmosphere (by respiration and combustion) at the same rate as it left it (by photosynthesis and dissolving in the oceans)

    b carbon dioxide was added to the atmosphere faster (by respiration and increasing combustion) than it left it (by photosynthesis and dissolving in the oceans)

C4.6

A more, fossil, deforestation, radiation, warmer / hotter, greenhouse effect, higher / greater, global warming, climate, weather

B **a** 3   **b** 1   **c** 2   **d** 4

C 1, 6, 3, 4, 2, 5, 7

D e.g., primary impact – more frequent droughts, secondary impact – crops fail; primary impact – ice melts, secondary impact – floods in coastal areas; primary impact – more storms, secondary impact – soil erosion / landslips / buildings and infrastructure destroyed

C4.7

A processing, reduced / lower, pollution / noise / congestion

B 1, 6, 5, 4, 2, 3

C advantages – producing aluminium from recycling requires less energy than producing it from aluminium ore; recycling results in less waste solid than producing it from ore; supplies of aluminium ore will last longer; disadvantages – some people do not like sorting their waste, and the lorries that collect cans for recycling produce polluting / greenhouse gases; overall judgement given, with reasons

D similarities – both involve collection; both involve separating different materials from each other; both involve making shreds; both involve melting and then cooling so that the material solidifies / freezes differences – magnets are used to sort different types of can, but colour and density are used to sort different types of plastic; recycled plastics are initially made into small pellets, but aluminium is made into large ingots

C2 Chapter 4 Pinchpoint

A this is an incorrect answer – both melting and **freezing** are involved in the formation of igneous rock from any starting material

B this is the correct answer

C this is an incorrect answer – when a metamorphic rock is formed as a result of the action of heat on existing rock, the existing rock **does not melt**; its particles are rearranged only

D this is an incorrect answer – **igneous rock** is formed as a result of existing rock melting and freezing; **sedimentary rock** is formed as a result of weathering, transport, sedimentation, and compression or cementation

Pinchpoint follow-up

A 1, 5, 6

B The conversion of metamorphic rock to igneous rock involves **melting** and freezing. Sedimentary rock may be formed from igneous rock by these processes occurring in this order: weathering, **transport**, **sedimentation**, cementation. The conversion of **sedimentary** rock to **metamorphic** rock involves the rearrangement of particles as a result of the action of heat or high pressure. The conversion of igneous rock to sedimentary rock may involve these processes occurring in this order: **weathering**, **transport**, sedimentation, compression. Metamorphic rock may be formed from igneous rock as a result of the action of **high** pressure. Sedimentary rock forms igneous rock when it **melts and then freezes**. Igneous and **metamorphic** rock consist of crystals.

C a 4, 7, 3, 8, 2, 6, 5, 1
   b rock is broken up to make small pieces of rock – sedimentary; rock is heated. It does not melt, but its particles are rearranged – metamorphic; rock is heated. It melts and freezes again – igneous; rock experiences high pressures. Its particles are rearranged – metamorphic

D igneous – melting, freezing; metamorphic – action of high pressure makes particles rearrange, action of high temperature makes particle rearrange without melting; sedimentary – transport, cementation

C2 Revision Questions

1 **four** from: atmosphere [1], oceans [1], sedimentary rocks [1], fossil fuels [1], plants and animals [1], soil [1]

2 a sugar [1]   b 102 g – 95 g [1] = 7 g [1]

3 a a material that water can soak into [1]
   b there are small gaps between the sediments that the rock is made from [1]

4 copper and silver nitrate solution [1]; magnesium and copper chloride solution [1]

5 a add small pieces of each metal to big trough of water [1] and observe vigour of reaction – the metal that reacts most vigorously is most reactive; control variables – size of metal [1], volume / amount of water [1]
   b **one** from: place a protective screen between reaction vessel and class [1]; do not touch the metals [1]

6 a the sedimentary rock melts [1] and freezes [1]
   b the igneous rock is weathered [1] and the resulting sediments transported [1]; sedimentation then occurs [1] followed by compaction or cementation (to make the sediments join together) [1]

7 $4Li(s) + O_2(g) \rightarrow 2Li_2O(s)$ [1 for correct balancing, 1 for correct state symbols]

8 composition – both are made from iron and nickel [1]; properties – inner core is solid, so cannot flow [1]; outer core is liquid, so can flow [1]

9 strength of wood-reinforced poly(ethene) is 32 MPa and strength of glass-reinforced poly(ethene) is 86 MPa [1]

glass-reinforced poly(ethene) is $\frac{86\,MPa}{32\,MPa} = 2.7$ times stronger than wood-reinforced poly(ethene) [1]

10 igneous – liquid rock freezes / solidifies to make crystals [1]; metamorphic – particles in existing solid rock are rearranged to form solid crystals [1] by the action of heat or pressure [1]

11 e.g. rising mean global temperatures leads to melting ice [1] and flooding of low-lying land [1]; **or** rising mean global temperatures leads to climate change, including more frequent droughts in some areas [1] which may lead to crop failures [1]

12 a $\frac{45}{500} \times 100$ [1] = 9% [1]
    b i carbon dioxide [1]   ii one of the products is a greenhouse gas / contributes to global warming / contributes to climate change [1]

13 from top – a pure element; a mixture of two compounds; a mixture of an element and a compound; a mixture of two elements [3 if all correct; 2 if 2 or 3 correct; 1 if 1 correct]

14 in Group 1, melting point decreases from top to bottom [1] but in Group 0, it increases from top to bottom [1]; all the Group 1 elements conduct electricity [1] but none of the Group 0 elements do [1]; the Group 1 elements are very reactive [1] but the Group 0 elements are unreactive / inert [1]

15 a rubidium chloride [1]   b rubidium [1]
    c reactivity increases from top to bottom of Group 1, so rubidium is the most reactive of the elements given [1]
    d $2Rb + Cl_2 \rightarrow 2RbCl$ [2; 1 for correct symbols, 1 for correctly balanced]

16 a Y [1]   b Y has typical ceramic properties (including high melting point, brittle, electrical insulator) [1]
    c Z [1]   d **one** from: flexible [1], low density [1]

P1.1

A protons, electrons, neutral, friction, electrons, negatively, electric field, repel, attract, lightning

B a friction, electrons, electrons, positive, negative
   b A – repel; B – attract; C – attract; D – repel

C a paint droplets lose electrons
   b i paint droplets attracted to car
      ii more paint adheres to the car / less paint is wasted

D similarity: both get weaker with distance; both produce non-contact forces; both are invisible
   difference: electric field affects charge, gravitational field affects mass; electric fields produce forces that can attract or repel charges, but gravitational fields produce forces which can only attract masses

P1.2

A electrons, second, ammeter, series, ammeter, amp, A, cell, battery (either order), motor, switch, complete

B a   b series

   c movement of charge (or charged particles); amount of charge flowing per second

C decreases

D a i charge   ii the speed of the rope
   b same number of charges in the circuit, but they are now moving more slowly

P1.3

A potential difference, voltmeter, parallel, volts, V, voltage, rating, high / large, energy, low / small

B **a**

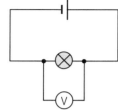

b cell, voltage, cell, volts

C current – same – charge; potential difference – total – energy
D increases
E ammeter measures the current passing through it so needs to be in the path of the current, that is 'in series'; voltmeter measures the amount of energy transferred between two points, so is connected across those two points or 'in parallel' with them

P1.4

A series, smaller, current, potential difference, potential difference, parallel, larger, current, current, potential difference

B **a** 6V **b** 0.8A **c** 6V

C parallel; so that you can switch off any one socket and others still work

D series – amount of charge flowing into and out of every component must be the same so current must be the same everywhere; parallel – amount of charge flowing through the cell must equal the total amount of charge flowing into the branches, so the current through the cell must equal the total current into the branches

P1.5

A resistance, potential difference, current, ohm, resistance, high, low

B $\frac{6.0}{0.20} = 30\,\Omega$

C **a** $current\ (A) = \frac{potential\ difference\ (V)}{resistance\ (\Omega)}$ **b** $\frac{9.0}{30} = 0.30\,A$

D **a** potential difference (V) = current (A) × resistance (Ω)
   b $0.50 \times 20 = 10\,V$

E moving electrons (charges) colliding with vibrating metal ions (atoms) as they pass along the wire

F length – increases – more vibrating particles;
diameter – decreases – more paths

G resistance of coating is greater than resistance of wire; wire needs to allow charges to pass / current to flow; coating must not let current flow or person get shock

P1.6

A magnets, magnetic materials, iron, iron, north pole, south pole (either order), north, Earth's, south, different, same, magnetic field, magnetic field lines, more

B **a** attract **b** attract **c** repel **d** repel

C pair of magnets at top of bag need to have different poles facing each other (e.g. N facing a S) because opposite poles attract, closing the bag

D **a**

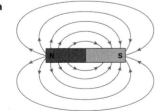

b S, stronger – near either pole of magnet; W, weaker – far from either pole
c magnetic field is stronger

E hang / suspend the magnet so that it can spin freely; its north pole will point in the desired direction

P1.7

A coil, turns / loops, core, more turns, current, material, magnetise, permanent, turned off, field, bar

B current, coil, core, magnetic field, current, doesn't

C **two** from: increase number of turns on the coil; increase current flowing in the wire / increase the power supply potential difference; use a magnetic material in the core

D increase current – stronger – charges moving more generates a stronger field; remove magnetic core – weaker – particles of air are not magnetic, so do not line up to strengthen field; decrease number of turns on coil – weaker – fewer turns adding to field; reverse direction of current – no difference – just exchanges poles

P1.8

A motor, coil, permanent magnets, current, electromagnet, spin / move, relay, larger, circuit, electromagnet, magnetised, completing / closing, safety

B 2, 1, 3, 4

C iron bar will pick up magnetic materials when switch is closed, won't pick up non-magnetic ones; need switch so that can drop them into another pile to separate them when switch is opened

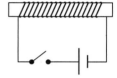

D **a** turns slower **b** turns faster **c** turns faster

E switch in series with single cell, connected to sides of relay; X-ray machine in series with many cells connected to ends of relay

P2 Chapter 1 Pinchpoint

A this is an incorrect answer – current is **not** 'used up' by components

B this is an incorrect answer – the bulbs are **dimmer** in the series circuit because it has higher resistance

C this is an incorrect answer – the potential difference across each bulb in the parallel circuit is the **same** as that of the cell, whereas the p.d. across the cell is **split** between the two bulbs in the series circuit

D this is the correct answer

Pinchpoint follow-up

A created, destroyed, same, flowing, second, same, current

B **a** increase **b** decrease **c** lower **d** same

C **a** a measure of the push of a cell or battery, or the energy that the cell or battery can supply
   b **i** potential difference tells you how much energy can be transferred to a circuit
   ii the potential difference across all branches of a parallel circuit must be the same
   iii any one electron must do the same work on the components as the battery did on it
   iv the p.d. across each branch in a circuit is always equal to the p.d. across the cell

D **a** 1.5V; parallel circuit so 3.0V across each branch, two identical components in series, so same p.d. across each so they add up to 3.0V
   b 0.6A; parallel circuit so current through both branches together must add up to 1.2A; branches are identical, so same current through each branch; as the two bulbs in each branch are in series, the current is the same through each bulb

P2.1

A energy, joule, kilojoule, activities, fat

B **a** sleeping 300; working 600; running 3600
   b sleeping involves no exercise but running involves a lot, so requires more energy

C **a** $20 \times 300 = 6000\,kJ$
   b anything that adds up to previous answer, e.g. 400g of chicken breast, 400g of pasta, 100g of banana, 110g of apple
   c **i** $300 \times \frac{160}{2} = 24\,000\,kJ$
   ii 1.3kg of dried fruit & nut mix or 1.6kg of chocolate

D walking: $1 \times 800 = 800$; working: $6 \times 600 = 3600$;
relaxing: $5 \times 360 = 1800$; sleeping: $12 \times 300 = 3600$; total: 9800 kJ

P2.2

A conservation, energy, energy stores, fill, total, chemical, thermal, kinetic, gravitational potential, elastic, dissipated

B **a** chemical store – coal fuel (and oxygen in air); thermal store – water; thermal store – surroundings

   b chemical store – fuel in car (and oxygen in air); kinetic store – car; thermal store – car and surroundings

   c gravitational potential store – Charlie and scooter; kinetic store – Charlie and scooter; thermal store – scooter wheels and ground

C **a** **i** gravitational store of skier, fills; chemical store of fuel, empties; thermal store of surroundings, fills

   ii thermal store of surroundings

   b **i** power station transfers energy to the lift using electrical current

   ii chemical store of coal empties by as much as the gravitational store of the lift and people fills

D left lid off saucepan – systematic – put lid on; thermometer reading – random – read thermometer at eye level each time; timing – random – repeat experiment three times

P2.3

A temperature, thermometer, degrees Celsius, °C, same, equilibrium, no, more, thermal, mass, type (either order)

B **a** °C, stays the same, increases, move / vibrate, J, thermal, increases   **b** less, hotter, more

C water, much larger mass

D **a** no – the person is warmer than their surroundings

   b yes – tea has cooled to same temperature as room

   c yes – thermometer has warmed to same temperature as mouth

P2.4

A thermal, hot, cooler / colder / cold, vibrate, conduction, solid, gaseous / gas, dense, dense, convection, convection current

B **a** particles heated, vibrate more; collide with neighbours and make them vibrate more; energy transferred from hotter place to colder place

   b 4, 1, 2, 3

C gases, thermal, far apart, weak, solids, non-metals, solids, gas

D steel is a metal, very good thermal conductor, very poor insulator, liquid heats fastest; polystyrene is mostly air, a gas and good insulator so liquid not heated as fast; plastics are insulators and a vacuum has no particles to transfer energy, very good insulator and so liquid heats slowest

P2.5

A conduction, convection, radiation, infrared radiation, thermal imaging camera, absorb, transmitted / absorbed / reflected (any order) × 3, black (or dark), matt (or dull), white (or light), shiny / gloss, black, matt

B **a** conduction – particles vibrating; convection – particles moving; radiation – emission and absorption of infrared

   b hot objects emit infrared radiation; when an object absorbs this radiation, it causes heating

   c radiation reaches the Earth from the Sun through space, where there are no particles / which is a vacuum

C large area due to the fins; dull (black) finish

D leave equipment in place to cool after the experiment

P2.6

A energy resource, fossil fuels, non-renewable, thermal power station, renewable, carbon dioxide, sulfur dioxide

B **a** natural gas, biogas   **b** 2, 5, 1, 4, 6, 3

C e.g. renewables – will never run out; do not produce greenhouse gases; do not contribute to global warming; do not produce acid rain; produce little waste; need no 'fuel' so cheap to run; non-renewables – historically tended to be cheaper; a lot of energy per kg of fuel; reliable

D all distance measurements too small; a systematic error because the results are all changed in the same direction

P2.7

A energy, time, energy, power, current, potential difference (either order), power rating, watt, kilowatt, kilowatt hour

B **a** $\dfrac{45\,000}{30} = 1500$ W

   b **i** $10 \times 230 = 2300$ W   **ii** $2300 \times 30 = 69\,000$ J or 69 kJ

   c $2 \times 4 = 8$ kW h

C **a** cost = power × time × cost per unit

   $= \dfrac{75}{1000} \times (4 \times 365) \times 15 = 1643$ p

   b cost = power × time × cost per unit

   $= \dfrac{11}{1000} \times (4 \times 365) \times 15 = 241$ p

   c £16.43 − £2.41 = £14.02

P2.8

A work, energy, done, joule, force, work, energy, simple machines, levers, gears (either order)

B **a** $120 \times 0.40 = 48$ J

   b 48 J (same as for **a**), because machines conserve energy

C **a** work done = force × distance = $1500 \times 1.0 = 1500$ J

   b work done = $30 \times 50 = 1500$ J

   c Ethan's chemical store empties, and the gravitational store of the load fills, as does the thermal store of Ethan's body and the surroundings; the amount lost from the chemical store is equal to the total gain in the gravitational and thermal stores

P2 Chapter 2 Pinchpoint

A this is an incorrect answer – a store of energy cannot just be 'used up'

B this is the correct answer

C this is an incorrect answer – the battery does not store electricity, it has a store of **chemical energy**

D this is an incorrect answer – the thermal store of the room **does not increase**; it **empties and fills at the same rate** so that it stays constant; it is the increase in the thermal store of the **surroundings** that is equal to the loss from the chemical store

Pinchpoint follow-up

A **a** warmer, heated, empties, fills, fill

   b constant, empties, rate, fills, warmer

B increases temperature difference between inside of house and surroundings; house heats surroundings faster; over one hour, thermal store of surroundings fills more

C work, store, chemical, fuel, thermal, water, chemical, fuel, chemical, dissipation, surroundings

D **a** true   **b** false   **c** true
   d false   **e** true   **f** true

P3.1

A speed, distance, metre(s) per second, distance, speed, speed, instantaneous speed, average speed, relative motion, relative speed, relative speed

B   **a** $\dfrac{500}{30} = 17\,\text{m/s}$ (to 2 sig. fig.)   **b** $\dfrac{160}{2.0} = 80\,\text{km/h}$ (to 2 sig. fig.)

   c $330 \times 12 = 4000\,\text{m}$ (to 2 sig. fig.)

C   **a** $\text{speed} = \dfrac{\text{distance}}{\text{time}} = \dfrac{20\,\text{m}}{0.5\,\text{s}} = 40\,\text{m/s}$

   b   yes, it was breaking the speed limit

D   **a**   the relative speed of the airliner compared to the ground is the difference in speeds between these two objects;

   b $900 + 110 = 1010\,\text{km/h}$

P3.2

A distance–time, horizontal, speed, accelerating

B   **a**   **i**   0.00; 0.04; 0.12; 0.28; 0.44; 0.60; 0.76; 0.80; 0.81

     ii

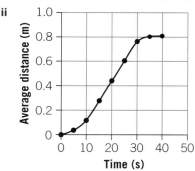

   b   **i**   the toy starts stationary; it accelerates for 10 s

     ii   it moves at its fastest, constant speed for 20 s

     iii   it then slows to a stop in 10 s

   c   speed = 0.032 m/s (to 2 sig. fig)

P3.3

A gas pressure, particles, compressed, density, atmospheric pressure, atmospheric pressure, smaller / less

B temperature – increase – gas particles move faster; volume – decrease – particles have further to travel

C if the can is heated, the particles inside will move faster, colliding with the container harder and more often, causing a larger pressure; large difference in pressure compared to outside pressure might explode the can

D kick a football further – air particles collide with objects less often; cannot run as far – less oxygen per litre; speed of sound is lower – neighbouring air particles

E air pressure decreases with altitude; at 10 km, it is so low it would kill the passengers because they would not be able to get enough oxygen from each breath, so they keep the pressure high enough that it is not dangerous

P3.4

A liquid pressure, pressure, upthrust, density, incompressible

B   **a**   upwards arrow from where ship touches water labelled upthrust (or buoyancy); downwards arrow from same place, same length, labelled weight (or gravity)

   b   upwards short arrow from middle of anchor labelled upthrust (or buoyancy); downwards long arrow from same place labelled weight (or gravity)

C as you go deeper in the ocean, pressure increases; as you go deeper, there is more weight of water above you, so since pressure = force/ area, the pressure must get larger

D   **a**   float; large volume of gas with low density means average density is less than water

b gas is compressible, but water is not; high pressure means that the air in the lungs shrinks, collapsing the lungs, increasing the diver's average density

E water pressure increases with depth; storing the water 40 m above ground means the pressure in pipes at ground level is the equivalent to a 40 m depth

P3.5

A pressure, force, surface area, newtons per square metre, force, pressure, large, small, pressure, larger, less

B   **a** $\dfrac{5.0}{0.010} = 500\,\text{N/m}^2$ **b** $\dfrac{2500}{6.4} = 390\,\text{N/m}^2$ (to 2 sig. fig.)

C   **a**   weight = mass × gravitational field strength
     $= 78 \times 10 = 780\,\text{N}$

   b $\text{area} = \dfrac{780\,\text{N}}{2800\,\text{N m}^2} = 0.28\,\text{m}^2$

D   **a**   large paws on lynx mean lower pressure on ground, so less likely to sink into snow, making it easier to move around; this is less important to the bobcat because it rarely lives with snow

   b   sharp means small area, so large pressure to push into the surface; large head means small pressure so you do not hurt your thumb

P3.6

A pivot, moment, moment, force, distance, pivot, newton metre, force, pivot, moment, equilibrium, law of moments, weight, above, below (either order), no, topple

B   **a** $5.0 \times 0.50 = 2.5\,\text{N m}$ **b** $50 \times 0.40 = 20\,\text{N m}$

   c   so there is no turning moment due to their weight, so they do not topple off the rope

C   **a** $\text{force} = \dfrac{\text{moment}}{\text{distance}}$

   b   **i** $\text{force} = \dfrac{10\,\text{N m}}{0.110\,\text{m}} = 91\,\text{N}$

     ii   yes, as the force required is less than the force she can exert

P2 Chapter 3 Pinchpoint

A this is an incorrect answer; Daisy is **moving** with a constant speed

B this is an incorrect answer; Daisy is accelerating and so her speed is **changing**

C this is the correct answer

D this is an incorrect answer; Daisy is moving with a constant speed, so is **not** accelerating

Pinchpoint follow-up

A   **a**   distance travelled, time taken, no / zero, zero, level

   b   **i**   horizontal line

     ii   starting horizontal and curving upwards

B   **a**   slope, speed, steep, shallow, changing, curve

   b   **i**   straight, diagonal, shallow, upward line

     ii   straight, diagonal, steep, upward line

     iii   starting horizontal and curving upwards

C   **a**   50 s to 100 s   **b**   100 s to 200 s   **c**   0 s to 50 s

D   **a**   unbalanced, change, constant, constant, cannot

   b

   c   **ii** and **iii**

P2 Revision Questions

1 **a** charge [1]   **b** $\dfrac{12}{4.0} = 3.0$ [1] Ω [1]

   c wire – conductor [1]; wrapping – insulator [1]

2 **a** $\dfrac{1200}{20} = 60$ [1] W [1]

   b **i** $\dfrac{60}{1000} = 0.06$ (kW) [1]

      ii cost (p) = power (kW) × time (h) × cost per unit (p / kWh) [1]
           = $0.06 \times 2 \times 15$ [1] = 1.8 p [1]

3 **a** standing still / stationary / not moving [1]

   b axes with reasonable scales (time on x-axis, distance on y-axis) [1], accurately plotted points [1], joined point-to-point with straight lines: straight diagonal line from 0 s, 0 m up to 120 s, 180 m; horizontal line across to 180 s, 180 m; straight diagonal line up to 300 s, 280 m [1]

   c speed $= \dfrac{\text{distance}}{\text{time}} = \dfrac{180}{120}$ [1] = 1.5 [1] m/s [1]

4 **a** $200 \times 3000 = 600\,000$ [1] J [1]

   b larger [1], doing more work / exercise [1]

5 **a** temperature [1], volume [1]   **b** pressure $= \dfrac{\text{force}}{\text{area}}$ [1]

   c **i** $1.8 \times 0.5 = 0.90$ m^2 [1]

      ii $\dfrac{800}{0.90}$ [1] = 890 N/m^2 [1] (to 2 sig. fig.)

      iii no, he will not sink as 890 < 20 000 N/m^2 [1]

6 (from top) gravitational & electric [1]; gravitational [1]; electric [1]; gravitational & electric [1]; electric [1]

7 **a** increase [1] – larger current produces stronger magnetic field [1]

   b decrease [1] – each turn provides some magnetic field [1]

8 **a** conductor [1] – electrons free to move throughout metal [1]

   b insulator [1] – insulating material contains many trapped bubbles of air / gas [1]

9 **six** from: natural gas non-renewable [1], can run out [1], produces cheaper electricity [1] (or converse), emits carbon dioxide when used [1] which causes climate change / global warming [1]; wind renewable [1], cannot run out [1], not available all the time / unreliable [1], wind turbines noisy / unsightly [1]

10 electricity charged according to energy transferred [1]; energy transferred is power times time [1]; time to boil more powerful kettle is **less** than half [1]; although power doubled, bill will decrease slightly [1] or equivalent numeric argument: (3000×140) (J) < (1500×300) (J) [1]

11 **a** $\dfrac{30}{1000} = 0.030$ m [1]; $8.0 \times 0.030 = 0.24$ N m [1]

   b moment is force times distance [1]; hand provides moment at handle [1]; equal moment applies to blades [1]; moving object closer means smaller distance, so force gets larger and cuts more easily [1]

12 **a** incorrect [1] – liquids are not compressible [1]

   b incorrect [1] – surface at lower pressure than deep ocean [1]

   c correct [1] – surface at lower pressure than deep ocean [1]

Periodic table

key

relative atomic mass
atomic symbol
name
atomic (proton) number

1	2												3	4	5	6	7	0
					1 **H** hydrogen 1													4 **He** helium 2
7 **Li** lithium 3	9 **Be** beryllium 4												11 **B** boron 5	12 **C** carbon 6	14 **N** nitrogen 7	16 **O** oxygen 8	19 **F** fluorine 9	20 **Ne** neon 10
23 **Na** sodium 11	24 **Mg** magnesium 12												27 **Al** aluminium 13	28 **Si** silicon 14	31 **P** phosphorus 15	32 **S** sulfur 16	35.5 **Cl** chlorine 17	40 **Ar** argon 18
39 **K** potassium 19	40 **Ca** calcium 20	45 **Sc** scandium 21	48 **Ti** titanium 22	51 **V** vanadium 23	52 **Cr** chromium 24	55 **Mn** manganese 25	56 **Fe** iron 26	59 **Co** cobalt 27	59 **Ni** nickel 28	63.5 **Cu** copper 29	65 **Zn** zinc 30		70 **Ga** gallium 31	73 **Ge** germanium 32	75 **As** arsenic 33	79 **Se** selenium 34	80 **Br** bromine 35	84 **Kr** krypton 36
85 **Rb** rubidium 37	88 **Sr** strontium 38	89 **Y** yttrium 39	91 **Zr** zirconium 40	93 **Nb** niobium 41	96 **Mo** molybdenum 42	[98] **Tc** technetium 43	101 **Ru** ruthenium 44	103 **Rh** rhodium 45	106 **Pd** palladium 46	108 **Ag** silver 47	112 **Cd** cadmium 48		115 **In** indium 49	119 **Sn** tin 50	122 **Sb** antimony 51	128 **Te** tellurium 52	127 **I** iodine 53	131 **Xe** xenon 54
133 **Cs** caesium 55	137 **Ba** barium 56	139 **La*** lanthanum 57	178 **Hf** hafnium 72	181 **Ta** tantalum 73	184 **W** tungsten 74	186 **Re** rhenium 75	190 **Os** osmium 76	192 **Ir** iridium 77	195 **Pt** platinum 78	197 **Au** gold 79	201 **Hg** mercury 80		204 **Tl** thallium 81	207 **Pb** lead 82	209 **Bi** bismuth 83	[209] **Po** polonium 84	[210] **At** astatine 85	[222] **Rn** radon 86
[223] **Fr** francium 87	[226] **Ra** radium 88	[227] **Ac*** actinium 89	[261] **Rf** rutherfordium 104	[262] **Db** dubnium 105	[266] **Sg** seaborgium 106	[264] **Bh** bohrium 107	[277] **Hs** hassium 108	[268] **Mt** meitnerium 109	[271] **Ds** darmstadtium 110	[272] **Rg** roentgenium 111	[285] **Cn** copernicium 112		[286] **Nh** nihonium 113	[289] **Fl** flerovium 114	[289] **Mc** moscovium 115	[293] **Lv** livermorium 116	[294] **Ts** tennessine 117	[294] **Og** oganesson 118

*The lanthanides (atomic numbers 58–71) and the actinides (atomic numbers 90–103) have been omitted.

Great Clarendon Street, Oxford, OX2 6DP, United Kingdom

Oxford University Press is a department of the University of Oxford.
It furthers the University's objective of excellence in research,
scholarship, and education by publishing worldwide. Oxford is a
registered trade mark of Oxford University Press in the UK and in
certain other countries

British Library Cataloguing in Publication Data
Data available

978-1-38-203012-0

10 9 8 7 6 5

Paper used in the production of this book is a natural, recyclable
product made from wood grown in sustainable forests.
The manufacturing process conforms to the environmental regulations
of the country of origin.

Printed in China by Shanghai Offset Printing Products Ltd

Acknowledgements

Cover image: Anekoho/Shutterstock; **p91**: tlorna/Shutterstock;
p92: Shutterstock

All artwork by Aptara Inc., Q2A Media Services Ltd., and Phoenix
Photosetting